Collaborative
Library Design

ALA Editions purchases fund advocacy,
awareness, and accreditation programs
for library professionals worldwide.

Collaborative Library Design

From Planning to Impact

PETER GISOLFI

Chicago | 2018

PETER GISOLFI is the senior partner of Peter Gisolfi Associates, Architects and Landscape Architects, which is based in Hastings-on-Hudson, New York, and New Haven, Connecticut. Over the last thirty years as a practicing architect, he and his firm have built more than forty libraries—community libraries, school libraries, and college libraries. He is also a professor of architecture and landscape architecture at the City College of New York. His articles and essays have been widely published. His book *Finding the Place of Architecture in the Landscape* (2008) expresses his ideas about architecture and landscape architecture and their relationship to setting.

Extensive effort has gone into ensuring the reliability of the information in this book; however, the publisher makes no warranty, express or implied, with respect to the material contained herein.

ISBN: 978-0-8389-1717-6 (paper)

Library of Congress Cataloging in Publication Control Number: 2018010855

♾ This paper meets the requirements of ANSI/NISO Z39.48–1992 (Permanence of Paper).

Printed in the United States of America

22 21 20 19 18   5 4 3 2 1

DEDICATION

RUMORS THAT THE DIGITAL REVOLUTION WOULD LEAD INEVITABLY TO THE DEMISE OF LIBRARIES have proved untrue, as today's vibrant institutions can attest. Academic libraries have become places where people can explore, learn, and collaborate. Public libraries no longer serve simply as quiet, inspirational places to store books. They have emerged as community cultural centers, where spaces for collaborative work, reading, and study coexist with spaces for meetings, social interaction, and performances of every type. School libraries promote collaborative practices to transform teaching and learning. Libraries are active, lively places. Libraries are relevant. Curiously, none of this was anticipated.

This book is dedicated to the visionaries who were part of a nationwide movement to change libraries from what they were to what they are becoming. This book also recognizes the librarians, administrators, boards of trustees, boards of education, and building committees that have brought these projects into being, as well as the patrons who have welcomed these libraries to their campuses and neighborhoods. Thank you for supporting libraries and acknowledging the contributions they make to our civic, cultural, and academic lives.

CONTENTS

ACKNOWLEDGMENTS

MANY PEOPLE CONTRIBUTED TO THE RESEARCH, DESIGN, WRITING, AND EDITING OF THIS BOOK.

- My appreciation goes to the essay writers—librarians, library board members, and administrators—who have demonstrated that each of their libraries came into being through an intensely collaborative process.
- The design teams of architects, landscape architects, and interior designers worked collaboratively with our clients on each of the buildings. Recognition goes to the photographers whose work captures the spirit of these ten libraries.
- Sandra Mintzes and Monica Lake made creative contributions to the design of this book.
- I appreciate Sara Bloom's persistence, her thoughtful suggestions, and her careful editing of the manuscript.
- Thank you to Jamie Santoro, an acquisitions editor at the American Library Association. I am grateful for her intelligent participation, and for her patience while guiding this project to completion.

INTRODUCTION
Collaborative Design

I RECENTLY VISITED A NEW BUILDING DESIGNED BY A PROMINENT FIRM OF ARCHITECTS THAT I respect. This building does not measure up to their usual standards. The program is complicated and the building appears to be many things at the same time—different bits and pieces that might satisfy the wishes of disagreeing factions. There is no clear or compelling idea. The whole is less than the sum of its disparate parts.

As I thought about the building, I was reminded of one of the first public school projects I had worked on early in my career. The architect who preceded me had designed a series of renovations—an overly ambitious music area, carved out of one of the lower floors, and corridor-seating areas comprised of orange-colored carpeting attached to plywood boxes. Certain constituencies may have been satisfied, but no overarching idea for transforming the building had emerged.

I always use the word "collaboration" when talking about the interaction between architects and the building's owners; this is a common refrain in my profession. But when I think of the word more precisely, it occurs to me that people may confuse collaboration with compromise: "If I get the music suite, you can have the carpeted lounge areas in the corridors." This is compromise—give-and-take that satisfies different interests. Collaboration, on the other hand, can be antithetical to compromise. Collaboration refers to agreement, to establishing clear goals and reaching them. A goal or objective may then inspire an architectural idea.

The Collaborative Design Process

How does a collaborative design process work? For every building project, the owner and the architect prepare a program of space requirements. This document usually is many pages long and is filled with carefully detailed information about size, adjacencies, mechanical and electrical requirements, furniture needs, and so on. In addition to the program of space requirements, it is essential to establish clear objectives. In contrast to the lengthy program of space requirements, only five or six objectives might be listed. It is not unusual to have a twenty-page program of space requirements and only a single page of objectives. Here are some examples of objectives:

- The library should be at the center of the school.
- In order to encourage participation, the academic program spaces and those for the arts and athletics should overlap; they should be visible to each other.
- In order to create the sense of a communal institution, the various parts of the student center should be transparent to each other.

The next part of the process involves choices. Since architects prepare the drawings and sketches, we have a lot of influence. To make the process collaborative, architects should show the building committee alternative solutions that can be evaluated. Evaluating the alternatives often results in modifications to the objectives. This is fine. As the collaboration progresses, we gradually move to a building plan or an architectural idea that relates to the owner's objectives.

Other considerations enter into the process. There are regulations. There is a physical context. There is a budget. There is a schedule. But objectives speak to vision, and collaboration requires that we create a building that belongs to the people for whom it was designed. As a student, I was inspired when Louis Kahn spoke of the "form of the building," which referred to the central idea. Such essential ideas come from understanding the vision and the objectives of the owner.

Consider Kahn's Yale Center for British Art in New Haven, Connecticut, one of my favorite buildings. Three key objectives *might* have been as follows: design a contextual building that respects the commercial and institutional characteristics of Chapel Street; incorporate high gallery spaces that evoke the spirit of great halls in English manor houses in which grand portraits were hung; and create a museum based on a series of calm, interconnected, and light-filled interior spaces that allow the artworks to be the primary visual interest. All of these hypothetical objectives were met, and because it is a Louis Kahn building, it is also carefully crafted and was designed with Renaissance proportions.

Objectives Determine Design

I am reminded of a situation at Hackley School in Tarrytown, New York. (See "Sternberg Library at Hackley School" in part II of this book.) At one point in the discussions having to do with a second-level connector from Raymond Hall (a classroom building) to Goodhue Memorial Hall (the library building), competing constituencies were at odds. Some advocated a bridge that would establish open-air ground-level access from Akin Common to the main quadrangle. Others felt it was essential to eliminate that connection in order to build additional classrooms. I worked out a plan that left a modest opening between the two quadrangles and, at the same time, provided some classroom space at the first-floor level. This proposal was a compromise to satisfy competing points of view.

Walter Johnson, then the head of Hackley School, pointed out that the compromise solution did not comply with an important objective for the campus—open connections between key outdoor spaces. This observation helped to steer the group back to collaborating rather than compromising.

We chose the second-level connector with open access at grade.

Another example is the Center at Maple Grove in Kew Gardens, Queens County, New York. Here, the director and the cemetery board envisioned a building that would be both secular and spiritual, a place that would link the community and the cemetery. From their vision, three specific objectives emerged: the sacred spaces—the chapel, the columbarium, and the family space—should relate to the cemetery landscape; the administrative and meeting spaces should relate to the Kew Gardens neighborhood; and the building should create a new gateway and connection from the adjacent neighborhood to the cemetery. These three objectives guided the most significant aspects of the design.

Collaboration: A Wider Context

Of the traditional arts, architecture is the one remaining practical art. Music, painting, and sculpture have been freed from the didactic constraints that once disciplined them. We can debate whether this has been beneficial or harmful. But it remains clear that architects are not solitary artists. We build for people. We build in a specific setting. And we build for a practical purpose. There need not be a conflict between listening to the people who use the building and satisfying some higher artistic purpose. The art—the architecture—is derived from understanding the objectives and collaborating in a way that transforms a vision into architectural ideas. True collaboration is a symbiosis of the setting for the project, the intentions of the users, and the design ideas of the architect. Buildings designed in this way are successful.

This book looks at a series of ten library design projects and considers thirty voices that contributed to the collaborative process: the library administrators, trustees, and board members who were instrumental in the planning of each project; the architects who designed the buildings; and the librarians who work in the buildings and understand the impact of change.

—*Peter Gisolfi*

PART I

Public Libraries

Entry to the Darien Library at the reading courtyard

The Planning Process

Planning the Darien Library of the Future

By **KIMBERLY D. HUFFARD**

WHEN WE FIRST STARTED THINKING ABOUT HOW TO PROVIDE NEW SER-vices to our community, we had no idea how long the process would take, how much it would cost, or how our ideas would be realized. We had no sense of the technology involved, or that we would end up pursuing Leadership in Energy and Environmental Design (LEED) certification. And we never could have imagined the extraordinary building into which we would eventually move.

The Darien Library had been a vital part of the local community since 1894. During its long history, it occupied a variety of locations, moving to its previous home in 1957. Under the strong leadership of library director Louise Berry, a supportive board of trustees, and with significant local community support, we added on to our building in 1974 and in 1984, expanding our offerings and developing a culture of exceptional customer service. We were consistently ranked by Hennen's American Public Library Ratings as among the country's top ten libraries.

In 2000, we began a long-range planning process to continue to improve and provide the best library services. The consensus was

that our community loved the library, but our users wanted more services and more space— space for books on easy-to-browse book stacks, an updated technology center, small office/home office support services, a larger children's room, a dedicated teen area, and more flexible program and meeting spaces. At the same time, we needed to continue providing the quiet spaces and information services that are the heart of any library.

A New Building for a New Vision

We realized that many of our ideas about new spaces and services could not be implemented in the old building, and these ideas represented a break from what most libraries were implementing at that time:

- No circulation desk, but a welcome desk and a self-check RFID system
- Lightweight reference desk with librarians who circulate to help patrons
- Horizontal and vertical transparency throughout the building
- Substantial art gallery
- Material-handling system
- Business center

As we investigated expansion, we understood that working within our old library was not the best way to achieve our new vision. Our motto became "Once in a lifetime, a community builds a library," and we wanted to deliver a library to our community that would stand for generations.

Once the decision had been made to build new rather than remodel, we investigated a number of architecture firms, seeking to find one that shared our vision to construct a significant public building at the center of our New England village. Our working partnership with the chosen architect and team was the most important element in the success of the project. The architects envisioned a "heavy" building that would be infused with light and transparency—a building that would be open and accessible while also projecting a solid, permanent presence. At the same time, we wanted the building to retain the small-town look and feel of the existing fifty-year-old library, which many of our users did not want to lose.

In a sense, the library staff designed the library from the inside out, space by space, while the architects designed the building from the outside in and from the ground up. We combined our vision of the next generation of library services with their clear vision of a library's strength, purpose, and role at the center of the community.

A glass wall between the art collection and the reference library maximizes transparency and maintains acoustical separation.

Building "A Palace for the People"

Early on, we agreed on the building's core structure—a three-floor library plus a mezzanine. It would have an active main level, classic library functions on the upper levels, and computer instruction, computers for public use, technical services, and a material-handling system on the lower level.

When the architect first proposed this idea, he referred to Charles McKim's 1887 design of the Boston Public Library, a "palace for the people" with a busy main floor and a grand staircase that invited people to the floors above. This idea of the grand staircase resonated with us and it anchored us to a hallowed library tradition. This idea also merged with our own reference point: Ray Oldenburg's vision of libraries as described in his 1991 book *The Great Good Place,* where he foresaw libraries as "the third place," the "heart of a community's social vitality, the grassroots of democracy."

With this perspective in place, we embarked on the essentials of the design phase. We were fanatical about making sure that every space in the new building would work exactly right—incorporating all that was new. We also committed early to a sustainable site and building, so we needed to incorporate these strategies into the design as well.

Our planning team of architects, librarians, and administrators visited some of the newly constructed and most innovative libraries in the country. As we studied these buildings, it allowed us to work together on the creative process, discussing direction and solidifying our design ideas. Our team also met at ALA annual conferences, where we were able to compile notes and observations that could work with our own ideas. We continued this collaborative approach throughout the schematic design phase and floor plans. The architects and administrators participated in every design meeting for the first three years of the project.

Many of the spaces we worked on together were new to us and at first we had difficulty visualizing them. The architects built a scale model so we could

View from the four-story atrium to the reference library

look at adjacencies, but in fact, we did our best work in full size. We secured the use of a local basketball court and sketched out the spaces so we could visualize them in a scale more familiar to us. We then worked together to refine the spaces, focusing on size and patron flow throughout the building.

A Library of the Future

Space by space, floor by floor, it all came together in a building we think is spectacular, in a building that pleases the community, a building that *Library Journal* named as one of five "must visit" buildings for anyone thinking about the future of libraries.

We wanted to build the first of the new libraries for our community, not the last of the old. We were looking to the future role that libraries would play and we needed an architect with that same vision. In the end, we formed a wonderful partnership between library staff and an architect whose skill, experience, and determination brought our vision to life—a "great good place" that will serve our community for generations.

Kimberly D. Huffard was a Darien Library trustee from 1999 to 2005, and president of the board of directors from 2006 to 2009. She was also chair of the capital campaign from 2005 to 2006, and cochair of the building committee from 2008 to 2010.

In the light-filled atrium, an open metal stair connects all four floors of the library.

The Design

Darien Library Relates to Its New England Setting

By **PETER GISOLFI**

THE NEW DARIEN LIBRARY DEFINES THE SOUTHERN end of the central business district in Darien, Connecticut. It is directly across the street from the historic Spring Grove Cemetery and is adjacent to the town's police station. The two-acre site was an abandoned car wash and gas station that had leaked fuel into the water table aquifer; the saturated zone of the aquifer begins at only six feet below ground level. The previous library of 23,000 square feet was located about half a mile north; it was one of the busiest libraries in Connecticut.

- Remediate the polluted site.
- Design a new library based on a detailed program of space requirements, with usable interior space of 48,000 net square feet.
- House a collection of 185,000 items.
- Design the new building to maintain the same size staff.
- Design an energy-efficient, LEED-certified building that uses no more energy than the previous library.
- Create a healthy, comfortable building.

Program Requirements

Early in the design process, the building committee established requirements for the new library:

Design Objectives

The building committee, in collaboration with the architects, established design objectives for the library, which evolved as we worked together:

- Emulate typical New England public buildings, with brick exterior walls and a slate roof.
- Create inspiring spaces for reading, study, and collaborative learning.
- Create an open floor plan with interconnected spaces that are transparent to each other both vertically and horizontally.
- Embrace new ideas about public libraries and accommodate changing priorities in the future.
- Intermingle seating and book collections, with no large areas devoted exclusively to stacks.
- Create a community cultural center for a variety of activities.

New Plan

The new Darien Library is a three-and-a-half-story building of 55,000 square feet with entrances on the Boston Post Road and from the reading court adjacent to the parking lot. This plan resembles a central hall house with entries on the east and west. The southern exposure overlooks the historic cemetery.

The library is organized with the conversational functions at street level—information desk, recent acquisitions, café, community auditorium, fiction, digital media, and the children's library. The lower level includes digital instruction space, technical services, the young adult area, the automated material-handling system, and about 7,000 net square feet of unfinished space for future expansion.

On the second floor are the more traditional library functions—nonfiction, reference, periodicals, special collections, and administration. The mezza nine includes spaces for individual and group study and a formal meeting room. The glass atrium connects all four stories and serves as an art gallery on the lowest level.

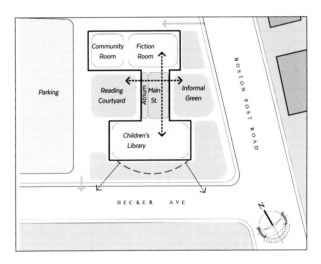

Conceptual plan diagram

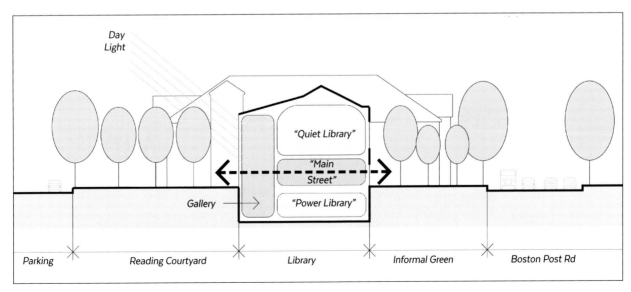

Conceptual building cross-section

Green Initiatives

The Darien Library is intrinsically sustainable, including:

- Well-insulated exterior envelope
- High thermal mass to stabilize the interior temperature
- Heating/cooling by four 1,500-foot "standing column" geothermal wells
- Energy consumption reduced when the building is unoccupied
- All interior spaces daylit
- Annual heating/cooling costs approximately the same as in the previous 23,000-square-foot building
- Native vegetation planted on-site
- Storm water from the roof and paving managed entirely on-site, with bioswales that filter the water
- LEED Gold certification

Collaborative Strategies

- The building committee included the library director and assistant director, members of the board of trustees, architects, landscape architects, mechanical engineers, green building consultants, and project manager. This committee met every two weeks.
- The other stakeholders included library staff, the board of trustees, Friends of the Library, planning board, selectmen, and community residents.
- One of the most interesting design debates focused on the four-story atrium. The architects originally designed a stair tower connected to a glass wall facing the reading court. To strengthen visible connections to the various levels, a member of the building committee suggested an open staircase directly behind the glass wall. Both schemes were drawn and mod-

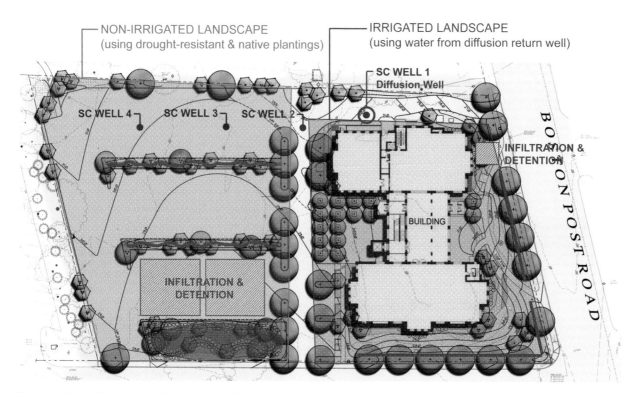

Sustainable landscape plan: the green-shaded landscape on the left uses drought-resistant and native plants that do not require irrigation; the blue-shaded landscape on the right uses water recycled from the geothermal wells for irrigation.

View from the reference library to the four-story atrium

eled, and it became clear that the open staircase supported the idea of transparency—one of the important objectives for the building.

Achieving Success: An Innovative Library

The Darien Library operates differently. There is no circulation desk; instead, an information desk is managed by one or two staff members. Patrons check out their books by means of an RFID system. Books are returned to kiosks located outside the building and in the entry foyer; these kiosks are connected to the automated material-handling system, which sorts the books for reshelving. There is no formal reference desk; librarians circulate within the collections to help patrons. The new library contains 48,000 square feet of occupied space and approximately 7,000 square feet of unfinished basement space that can be occupied in the future. The new library, which is more than twice the size of the previous 23,000-square-foot library, operates with the same size staff.

The Darien Library looks different from libraries of the past. The interior space is continuous and transparent, yet many of the spaces are intimate, clearly defined, and quiet. At the first level, the mood of the library is informal and conversational. Upstairs is quieter, traditional, more serene. The library is the main community cultural space for the town of Darien and its neighbors. It is a sustainable building, designed and constructed to last for generations.

Many of the qualities of the Darien Library were originally articulated by the library administrators and the building committee. From that dialogue, the basic objectives emerged and were met through a collaborative design process.

As an amusing aside, having reached consensus on major design issues involving millions of dollars, the collaborators could not agree on something as simple as color. After protracted discussion, it became necessary to appoint a committee of two—the chair of the board of trustees and the architect—to select the colors for all the spaces in the library. Sometimes, even the sacred collaborative process calls for a small decision-making team to move forward.

Nonfiction room on the south side of the library's second floor

"Main Street," on the first floor, encourages patron interaction and conversation

The Impact

Darien Library:
A Partner in Civic Initiatives

By **ALAN KIRK GRAY**

WHEN WE OPENED OUR NEW BUILDING, IT WAS immediately clear that our relationship to the community's library users had deepened and broadened. That first year, some of those in the community visited the New Darien Library, as we called it—already the busiest in the state on a per capita basis—as they had before: to find a book, or a DVD, or to do research. However, many residents found new reasons to become library users: to study, alone or with others, to meet friends at the café, perhaps to take part in the enhanced cultural and entertainment programs that the community room allowed us to present, or to dive into the Power Library—a suite of spaces with a range of new technology offerings, including a business center.

We opened just as the high school midterm finals were scheduled, and one teen, looking at the second floor Research Room with its expansive cherrywood tables and reading lamps, used a contemporary cultural image to exclaim, "This is just like Hogwarts. What a great place to study!" Someone a few years older told us she didn't have "anything this good at my college."

The new building provides a range of opportunities for contemplative use: quiet, tucked-away spaces, tables for groups of like-minded residents to pursue common interests, active technology clusters, and study and meeting rooms.

Visits to the library increased by 8 percent that first year.

Positive Changes in the New Building

Expanded shelving presented our collections in more accessible ways—some with a retail orientation, and others pulled together to allow research into collateral subjects. Though we opened the new building with fewer items in our collection, circulation increased by 17 percent. Patrons could find what they wanted easily, and they often found other items shelved nearby that called for their attention.

Our staff, empowered by technology such as the RFID-enabled materials management system that allowed self-checkout and self-return by patrons themselves, was able to devote more time to each user who sought assistance. Reference queries and reader advisory questions ("I like to read realistic historical fiction; what would you recommend I read next?") increased significantly—by 73 percent—and we found that the deeper engagement with our patrons increased the number of items checked out on each visit.

Moreover, the nature of visits to the library changed. Since the materials management system allowed drive-up returns, 40 percent of returns took place without a need to park and come into the building. As a result, fewer visits to the library were simply "transactional." Dwell time in the building increased since each visit was more likely to be for research, a study session, a meeting, or time in the enhanced technology spaces. Attendance at programs increased by 40 percent and the use of library computers increased by 63 percent.

Overall, the building's strength and obvious permanence—brick walls with deep-set windows, slate roof, light-filled spaces, timeless New England character—showed that we would be here on the Post Road, Darien's main west-to-east thoroughfare, for the next century.

Looking back on that first year, it is clear that our presence in the community has evolved substantially and fundamentally, in some ways as we had intended, and in some ways that we could not have foreseen.

In the old building, we were a well-liked local library, a friend to all who visited, and we were

In the small office/home office area on the lower level, computers are available for business support and instruction.

The auditorium on the first floor is in constant use for community events and programs.

important in the lives of those who chose to visit us. If we had expanded and refurbished the old building to meet increased demand, as we first intended, that probably would still be our role and place in the community—a comfortable place, continuing to be everyone's favorite neighbor. But we didn't go in that direction. Rather than build the last of the old libraries, we built one of the first of the new ones.

Traditional Library Offerings Are Enhanced

Some offerings are unchanged, as we had intended. As noted, use by individuals has increased substantially, as measured by circulation, questions asked and answered, computers used, and programs attended. As traditionally measured, our new building has made us a better library, where people can follow their passions, develop their interests, and improve their lives. And we still have that small-town, friendly feel, with a staff famous for its extraordinary patron service.

- Here in this building, toddlers make their first visit to a public building and start a pathway to a lifetime of literacy.

- Here in this building, we stay open late into the evening for students to study during midterms and finals. And they return to this building during holidays to study for the exams that await them back at their universities.

- Here in this building, senior citizens come to more programs than to any other organization in town, even those intended solely for their use.

- Here at the library, blood drives, Darien Health Department programs, Planning & Zoning public information sessions, and local hospital MedEd series all coexist with author programs, art lectures, and concerts. Book groups meet in the same rooms as neighborhood association groups.

- What we could not have predicted, though perhaps we might have hoped to see, was the role the new building has played in pulling people together, not as individuals, but as participating members of a community—a community of doers.

- More than a third of the 405 adult programs we provided last year represented a partnership with a local community organization, with each one taking place in the library because this is the place to go. Attendance at those programs was 31,494, in a town with a population of 20,000.

- Four times over the past eight years, storms have caused major losses of power in wide swaths of the town, and it was the library's building that provided shelter and community to those without heat and light, powered by a generator configured to run the entire building. Here is where the potluck suppers took place and where community leaders kept everyone up to date on progress to restore power.

- In this building, with its expansive, accessible spaces, the Darien Library plays a fundamentally important role in the town; it is used by nearly everyone, is universally respected, is a critical partner in nearly all civic initiatives, and it is the default place to go to for answers when the future is discussed.

DESIGN TEAM
Peter Gisolfi
Frank Craine
Cheng-hsun Wu
Ronen Wilk
Joori Suh

PHOTOGRAPHY BY
Robert Mintzes

The Building Belongs to Our Users

To be clear, our library does not provide the big answers, though we often provide needed information and context. We are providing the place—the physical and collaborative spaces, the meeting and study rooms, the community room, the conference room, and the tables by the café—where those questions are asked, addressed, spoken about, argued, and often resolved in groups large and small. In a community where the representative Town Meeting still holds the power of final decision, here at the library, democracy is at work in ways we could not have foreseen.

This is no longer our building, if it ever was. It belongs to our users. Whatever the future holds for this community, the Darien Library will play a role not only as a library, but also as a presence at the center of the community's engagement, spirit, and enterprise.

Alan Kirk Gray, formerly chief administrative officer of Darien Library, was named director in 2014.

Children's library on the south side of the building

South exposure in the children's library

New wing of the Longwood Public Library as viewed from the woodland to the south

The Planning Process

From a One-Room Schoolhouse to a 48,000-Square-Foot Building

By **GAIL LYNCH-BAILEY** *and* **KATHRINE SOSCIA**

PRIOR TO CONSTRUCTION OF THE FIRST LONGWOOD PUBLIC LIBRARY BUILDING in 1985 in Middle Island, New York, we had resided in a one-room schoolhouse in nearby Coram, in the Yaphank Education Center, and in two downtown storefronts. Crossing the threshold of our own building in 1985, we finally had plenty of space. Or so we thought . . .

For the next two decades, the Longwood Public Library grew—in numbers, knowledge, possessions, and patrons. A thousand people a day entered the library, and more would have come if they could have found parking and a place to sit. To the staff as well as library users, it became apparent that our building was inadequate for the needs of the community it served. We lacked room for books and materials as well as programs and people. Twenty years after moving in, we were bursting at the seams.

Every area of the library needed to expand. In the children's room, supplies were stacked on top of bookshelves. Space for parents and children to relax together was relegated to a tiny corner—which was too close, some felt, to the main entrance. There was no dedicated young adult space; a small corner carved out of the adult department was unsatisfactory for this growing population. Adults needed more seating, group study areas, and enhanced computer services. Patrons often had to wait in line to access a computer. The demand for program and meeting space soared. The community rooms were always booked, sometimes years in advance, and we lacked what many patrons desired—a true auditorium.

On top of all this—quite literally—the roof leaked and was in constant need of repair. Although we had added some solar panels where possible, the structure itself was not energy efficient. The building had few windows and could not take advantage of our recently purchased woodland property to the south. The place was dark; in fact, entire walls had been built without any windows at all. We needed more access to the outdoors, as well as ways to let in the restorative powers of light, air, and sunshine.

The Evolution of the Planning Process

The planning process for the Longwood Public Library's expansion and transformation evolved from a small group of people to eventually include professional experts and many representatives from the Longwood community. After initial conversations, the directors and the board of trustees took the first steps in planning in 2007 and 2008. Two community forums explored the future needs of the library. Using these meetings as the starting points for our project, the entire process took almost nine years.

Over the next two years, we conducted an internal needs assessment in every library department, and we produced a detailed report with the results. In addition, we completed a topographic survey of the library's properties. Armed with a PowerPoint

presentation about our need for space, the library's directors visited civic organizations and other key groups in the Longwood community. This outreach laid an important foundation for broader citizen involvement and eventual consensus.

During this time, the board put together a list of questions for architects. Prospective firms were researched and vetted. We sought and received feedback from other libraries that had completed similar projects. The board of directors then began to interview architects and construction managers.

In spring 2011, the Longwood Public Library retained a construction management company. The company began by preparing an "existing conditions" report about the library and followed up by interviewing various stakeholders in order to gauge the community's willingness to reinvest in the library. Equally important was the formation of a building committee, made up of key library staff, trustees, and experts in the construction field.

On June 10, 2011, the library hosted the first of two daylong community design meetings to set goals for the library project. All interested stake-

Longwood's new wing, south façade, and reading terrace at dusk

holders, including the construction managers and representatives from three architecture firms, were invited to participate. The goals outlined at the first meeting were used to steer the project design. At the second meeting, held a month later, each architecture firm formed two design teams of residents and library personnel and prepared a concept diagram for the renovation and expansion of the library. All six concepts were then presented to the entire group for consideration.

The following month, the board of directors and members of the building committee visited libraries and other buildings designed by the architects being considered. Following these visits, the team selected the architect for the project. Based on the needs assessment prepared previously by the library, the architects developed a schematic design for the building and site. The cost of this design was estimated by the construction managers and that became the budget included in the bond referendum that was passed on October 9, 2012. These collaborative efforts proved essential in the transformation of our library.

Advice for Library Leaders and Board Members

- Start early, maintain flexibility, and rely on research. The process may take considerably longer than expected, and some impatient taxpayers will question its validity along the way.
- Engage your library's key users and support groups. Seniors, students, and parents of young children recognized the benefits of expanding our library, and they outvoted the nonsupporters by a 2:1 ratio.
- Listen and be heard. Gather as much community and user input as possible.
- Never discard a suggestion until it is vetted. Insist that your architects, engineers, and contractors listen to you and respond to your concerns.

The new mezzanine overlooking the two-story reading room

- Hire qualified professionals with proven library design and building experience. This is not the time to give rookies the chance to establish themselves. Visit sites already completed by those you are considering and get feedback from the trustees and directors who hired them.
- Recognize that the process will be ongoing. Even with oversight by an excellent construction management firm, your work will continue, including bid notices and openings, special board meetings for awarding of contracts, as well as choices of furniture, fixtures, and finishes.
- Demonstrate fiscal responsibility and respect for the taxpayer. Under New York State law, public school and library budgets may not exceed an annual 2 percent increase or the inflation rate, whichever is lower. We pierced that cap only once, via special notice and voter approval. This prudence contributed to a successful project that was completed on time and on budget.

Gail Lynch-Bailey was president of the Longwood Public Library board from July 2015 to June 2016.

Kathrine Soscia was president of the Longwood Public Library board in 2012, and is the current president.

On the second floor, the reading alcove in the adult library looks south to the wooded landscape.

A Natural Landscape Suggests a Focus for the Longwood Public Library

By **PETER GISOLFI**

THE LONGWOOD PUBLIC LIBRARY IS LOCATED IN MID-dle Island on Long Island in New York State. The library shares the borders of the school district, and they jointly serve a population of 65,000. The placement of the library addresses diverse settings: it faces north toward Route 25, a busy state highway, and its southern boundary is a four-acre woodland.

Longwood Library was constructed in the 1980s on a tight budget. To save money, many windows were eliminated from the design. As a result, the second-floor community room had no windows and the adult library had narrow windows facing south, where a two-story stack area blocked views to the woodland. The building appeared to be a warehouse for books. Nevertheless, the library served the community well for thirty years. It was a gathering place of constant activity.

Program Requirements

The library staff provided the architects with a detailed program of space requirements, including the following key points:

- Increase the size of the building from 30,000 to 48,000 square feet.
- Create a vibrant teen area.
- Increase the size and importance of the children's library.
- Increase the size and variety of accessible public meeting spaces.
- Create a twenty-first-century public library, adaptable to future needs.

20

Alternative Concepts

In 2011, the newly appointed library director embarked on the campaign started by her predecessor to modernize and expand the library. A project management company was hired to organize design workshops called "charrettes" to engage design professionals and the community. Three architectural firms were invited to participate. The first charrette was for information gathering. During the second charrette, two architects from each firm led separate design teams that included a member of the library staff, a trustee, and several community stakeholders.

Working in the morning, each of the six teams produced a design scheme; these were presented to all participants in the afternoon. The scheme from the group I led was influenced by a walk I had taken with the former library director, during which we explored the woodland to the south. I understood immediately that the building should take advantage of that setting. Thus, our concept focused the library toward the woods and added a new wing to the west side of the building. That idea became the preferred plan and was selected by the planning team.

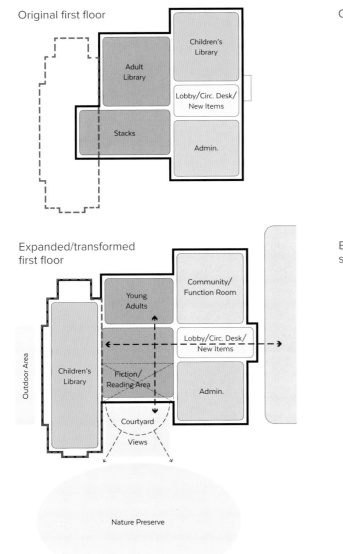

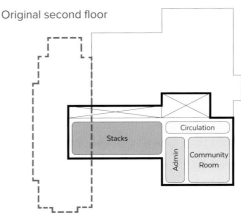

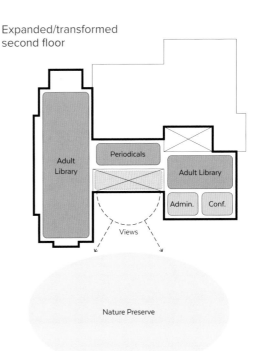

Objectives

The library board and professional staff collaborated with the architects to establish objectives for the design:

- Provide Middle Island with an active community cultural center.
- Connect the library visually to the natural landscape.
- Organize the building to be easily understood by the public.
- Create a civic presence on Route 25.
- Modify the building to be transparent and filled with daylight.
- Expand and reconstruct the building to be energy-conserving.

New Plan

As the previous diagram shows, the library's first floor is organized along an internal east-west pathway that begins at the newly enlarged entryway from the parking lot on the east and ends at the children's library in the new addition on the west. The north side of the pathway houses community rooms, the teen area, and digital instruction space; the south side includes an information desk and the new two-story reading room. An open stair connects the reading room to the second level, where administrative offices, quiet study areas, periodicals, and the adult library (in the new addition) all overlook the two-story space, which is the centerpiece of the library. Adjacent to the reading room is an outdoor reading terrace with views to the woodland.

The transformed building establishes a new dialogue with its setting. Throughout the building, generously sized windows add daylight and transparency, and a glass wall to the south faces the woods. Along Route 25, large-scale windows offer views of the newly installed sidewalk and street trees. The parking lot to the east was redesigned and planted with native vegetation. The entire site was reconfigured to manage storm water runoff in accord with current regulations. The library engages the site in new ways: the building connects to the "green" parking landscape on the east, to the wooded landscape on the south, and to the commercial landscape on the north.

The east entry has been transformed with more extensive glazing and a canopy. Inset: Original east entry.

A smaller circulation desk can be seen from the adjacent work room and from the second floor. Inset: Original circulation desk.

The new children's library is a spacious room with low stacks and ample daylight. Inset: Original cramped children's area.

New two-story reading room

To create an energy-efficient library, the entire building envelope was insulated; all windows are triple-glazed, and a new energy-saving heating and cooling system was installed. In 2017 the building received LEED platinum certification, the highest rating possible.

Collaborative Strategies

The designers, builders, and users of the building worked effectively together:

- The library director organized a building committee of key librarians, board members, and the head custodian. The members were engaged and outspoken.
- Periodically, the architects presented to the full library board. This group was insightful and articulate.
- During the construction phase, meetings with the building committee were held every two weeks. Materials and details were reviewed

multiple times to ensure that the intentions of the committee were met.

- When differences arose, a constructive consensus was reached. For example, many colors, finishes, and fabrics were sampled and evaluated before final choices were made.

Achieving Success

The expanded and transformed Longwood Public Library has exceeded its objectives. Four years of intense interaction demonstrate that an engaged board and a strong library director are essential for success. They set the scene for constructive collaboration.

The new building and landscape engage the physical setting—the street, the natural woodland, and the "green" parking lot. More subtly, the cultural iconography has been transformed: a box-shaped library with few windows has become an important civic building that embraces a varied suburban landscape.

True North, the new teen space, is north of the central reading room.

South-facing reading room and adjacent terrace

View from the stacks within the reading room
facing south to the wooded landscape

View from the second-floor mezzanine looking over the two-story reading room

The Impact

A Community Embraces the New Building

By **SUZANNE JOHNSON AND LISA JACOBS**

IN THE YEARS BEFORE THE LONGWOOD PUBLIC Library was transformed and expanded, our librarians faced vexing challenges. The demand for additional space was a daily contest for staff members looking to schedule programs. For instance, we had one large community room, which could be divided by a movable wall. But the space was not soundproof, so the cheerful laughs from the children's programs seeped into the quiet of yoga classes. There were no windows in the room and it was dreary. Nevertheless, an ever-growing number of PTA committees, scout troops, homeowners' associations, and other community groups competed for those spaces.

In addition, librarians lacked ample shelving for the collections and storage space for materials;

patrons lacked quiet spaces to work and comfortable seating, which had been jettisoned in favor of computers; and teens were relegated to a distant corner furnished with just a couple of tables. Change was needed.

Additional Space Allows Enhanced Programming and Services

The new library has been open for more than a year and many positive changes have benefited patrons of all ages, as well as the staff tasked with managing the daily activity in a busy library. Children's programs take place daily in the two new rooms created for them—a craft room and a storytime space. The additional space has allowed for new program ideas, such as a pop-up museum corner, study buddies, and a game called "Escape the Room." One young mother commented that the new spaces "feel like a second home for our children." Another said she was "totally in love with the new kids' area."

Tweens have their own area in which to hang out, away from younger siblings. Parents and caregivers can sit in comfortable chairs near the south side of the building and enjoy a magazine while their children search for books. Teen programs take place in their own dedicated space, where they can also use their computers, phones, and tablets to search for materials and information on their own. Civic groups are finding it easier to book space for their meetings. Computers are in use all day. Program attendance has increased dramatically.

The circulation of materials has undergone a major change. During construction, the entire collection was tagged for RFID. Three new self-checkout terminals were installed and the new circulation desk was reduced by half. The self-pickup of materials on hold was added as a labor-saving and time-saving convenience. As modern consumers, patrons expect these choices.

The lobby area has been outfitted with movable shelving and new books and DVDs are currently housed there. The shelving can be moved, which frees up the adjacent art gallery area for library events. The area offers casual seating and a coffee machine. The space is always occupied by patrons enjoying the sunny east exposure.

Practical Improvements for Librarians

The design of the new Longwood Public Library has benefited our librarians as well as the patrons we serve:

- The space for children's services has doubled and, for safety, the department is now located away from the front entrance and parking lot. Oversight is more manageable.
- With noisy activities clustered in appropriate spaces, separate from quiet work areas, the staff can be more creative in programming activities.
- Community meeting rooms have been relocated to the first floor, near the entrance, which makes it more convenient for attendees.

In the adult area on the second floor, natural light penetrates the building through north-facing clerestory windows.

- Energy efficiency, including triple-glazed windows, spray foam insulation, and daylight throughout the building, including offices and program rooms, makes the building more comfortable and cheerful for patrons and staff.
- Improved air quality and temperature control with upgraded heat and ventilation add to the indoor comfort for patrons and staff.
- During 2016, energy costs in the enlarged 48,000-square-foot building were less than the energy costs in the original 30,000-square-foot building.
- The building is transparent, improving wayfinding throughout the library.
- Access to the reading terrace provides quiet views of nature.
- Access to the adjacent natural area provides opportunities for new outdoor programming, including nature walks, bird watching, and exploration of the local flora and fauna.

DESIGN TEAM
Peter Gisolfi
Frank Craine
Kilung Hong
Ronen Wilk

PHOTOGRAPHY BY
Robert Mintzes

Walking through the expanded building, we are amazed at the diversity of individuals and groups using the library in different ways. People curl up in cozy chairs with a tablet, work at a small table on a laptop, or spread out their textbooks in a quiet study room. They collaborate quietly, or sit and gaze at the restful woodland view, or bask in the sun with the newspaper. They sit and play with their toddlers and post to social media on their phones. They browse the DVDs while their teens hunt for the best video games nearby. The list goes on . . .

One regular library user noted that the Longwood Public Library "is above and beyond on the outside and in." A retiree and daily user posted this Facebook review: "This is the best library I have ever experienced. The newly transformed and expanded building is amazing."

Suzanne Johnson was director of the Longwood Public Library from 2011 to 2016.

Lisa Jacobs is the current director of the Longwood Public Library and was assistant director from 2013 to 2016.

The new circulation desk is smaller and is visible to the work space and second floor.

The Planning Process

Planning an Expansion and Transformation of a Well-Loved Library

By **JANET C. LENTZ** *and* **ELOISE L. MORGAN**

BY THE 1990S, OUR 1942 LIBRARY, WHICH HAD BEEN DESIGNED TO EMULATE A graceful private house, was out of space and out of date. Following the passage of the American with Disabilities Act in 1990, the library's board of directors and professional staff evaluated a series of proposals to achieve at least partial compliance with the act, but they deferred construction while we considered a larger project to address other needs of the library.

By 1996, the Bronxville Public Library was one of only two libraries in Westchester County that was not handicapped-accessible. Our three-story structure had no elevator, its restrooms were two cramped spaces in the basement, and the aisles between book stacks were unacceptably narrow. You could not get into the building from either entrance without climbing a flight of stairs.

In addition to the lack of ADA accessibility, our building was just too small. The book collection had outgrown the available shelf space. It seemed that for every new book we added, we had to discard an older one. The popular children's room had insufficient space to satisfy programming needs, and its second-floor location was difficult to reach, especially for those with toddlers and strollers in tow. We had room for only three public computer stations and then only by wedging them awkwardly into the main entrance lobby. We had no dedicated place for a young adult collection. The staff was crowded into tiny work areas inconveniently located on the second floor. We had no central air-conditioning, the electrical service was outdated, the hardwood floors were warping, the windows were single-glazed, and we could go on . . .

In late 1996 we began a five-year process to update the Bronxville Public Library, spearheaded by Henry Doyle, president of the library board. As a first step, we engaged an experienced library planning consultant to evaluate our current situation and suggest ways to address the library's future needs. To assist in his work, our professional staff projected collection growth, and board members and others provided additional information based on experience and observation. The library board also conducted a community-wide survey to learn the public's views on the present and future use of the library.

In fall 1997, to no one's surprise, the consultant confirmed our long-held concerns about the lack of accessibility, inadequate space, and the need for physical plant upgrades. He noted, for example, that three staff members, computers, book trucks, boxes of new books, a copier, and files were crowded into a 100-square-foot area that was barely adequate for a one-person office. He also pointed out that while half of the library's circulation was children's mate-

rial, the children's room represented less than a quarter of the building.

Later that year, after interviewing several architects, we engaged Peter Gisolfi Associates to prepare preliminary diagrammatic floor plans, initial cost estimates, and exterior elevations for each of three options:

- A minimal scheme addressing ADA requirements, mechanical upgrades, and expansion of the children's room by adding approximately 2,500 square feet.
- A mid-range scheme providing the elements in the minimal scheme, but which would accommodate growth by adding approximately 6,000 square feet.
- A larger scheme accommodating all of the above, plus substantial growth by adding 8,000 to 10,000 square feet.

The restored reading room connects to a new reading porch.

Achieving the Best Results through Collaboration

Working in collaboration with the library board and library director, the architect spent early 1998 revising and refining the design options and developing cost estimates. After many revisions, the board of directors selected the medium-sized alternative, and we spent additional months working with the architect to further refine the design and cost estimates. In the end, due to a late decision to add a large community meeting room, we increased the building from 12,150 square feet to 20,650 square feet—a total of 8,500 square feet of additional usable space.

The Bronxville Public Library is funded by the village of Bronxville. Consequently, as cost estimates were developed in 1998, the library board and the village trustees jointly addressed the financing of the proposed project. We focused primarily on the sale of a valuable oil painting that had been bequeathed to the library in the 1940s. The painting was auctioned in December 1998 for $4.1 million, enough to underwrite the bulk of the construction budget. With that in hand, in early 1999, we contracted with the architecture firm for detailed construction drawings and other architectural services. The auction proceeds, when combined with a fund-raising campaign, allowed us to cover more than 90 percent of the cost of the project without public funding. Capital and operating budget funds made up the balance.

Throughout the process, our seven-member library board and the library director oversaw the planning and construction of the project. Several subcommittees took on the responsibilities for various aspects of the project: the building design, furnishings, the fine art collection, audiovisual equipment for the new community room, and landscaping, among others. During 1999 and 2000, the board's work on the project intensified: we hired a construction manager to represent the library's interests, we rented temporary library space and various storage facilities, we hired book and fur-niture moving companies, and we dealt with hundreds of details integral to each task. Construction bids were opened in February 2000, and we broke ground in April of that year. With a gala celebration, we reopened on September 9, 2001, presenting to the public a library that is 70 percent larger than the original, yet one that continues to retain its gracious residential character.

Advice for Those Preparing to Build or Expand Libraries

- Select professionals (architects, construction personnel, consultants) whose visions and work style are compatible with yours.
- Hire an experienced owners' representative to be your eyes, ears, and your boots on the ground.
- Strengthen the board of directors with members of applicable professional backgrounds and experience.
- Involve community members who have first-hand experience with handicap issues.
- Monitor the construction project daily and attend weekly meetings to resolve construction issues as they arise. Library board members and professional staff should be involved.
- Plan early for moving services and other contracts that may need to be competitively bid.
- Communicate, collaborate, cooperate. Keep all stakeholders informed from the early planning stages to the grand opening. Utilize social media, public meetings, local cable TV, press releases, newsletters, and village-wide mailings.
- Involve the library staff, not just the head librarian.
- Have fun. A project like this is a once-in-a-lifetime experience.

Janet C. Lentz joined the Bronxville Public Library board in 1994, and was president from 1997 to 2000

Eloise L. Morgan joined the Bronxville Public Library board in 1997, and was president from 2000 to 2004.

The Design

A Transformed Library Maintains the Original Vision

By **PETER GISOLFI**

THE BRONXVILLE LIBRARY OCCUPIES ONE CORNER of the village's key civic intersection. The other institutions that share the intersection are the Village Hall, the Bronxville School, and the Reformed Church. Together, the outdoor spaces of these four corners serve as an unconventional village green.

The original library of 12,150 square feet, completed in 1942, was designed by Harry Leslie Walker to resemble a grand, central hall house—a cultural institution for the community. It was a place for books, reading, and study, and was also an art gallery. The library serves the village of 6,400 people, plus a wider area of approximately 15,000.

Program Requirements

The building committee included the five-member library board and key members of the professional library staff. Together, they established guidelines for the project:

- Study three options for additional space (2,500, 6,000, and 8,000–10,000 square feet), based on the alternative programs of space requirements.
- Create a community room for music, lectures, concerts, drama, and public meetings.
- Double the size of the children's library.
- Create a generous young adult area.

Bronxville Library occupies the southeast corner of the village's main civic intersection.

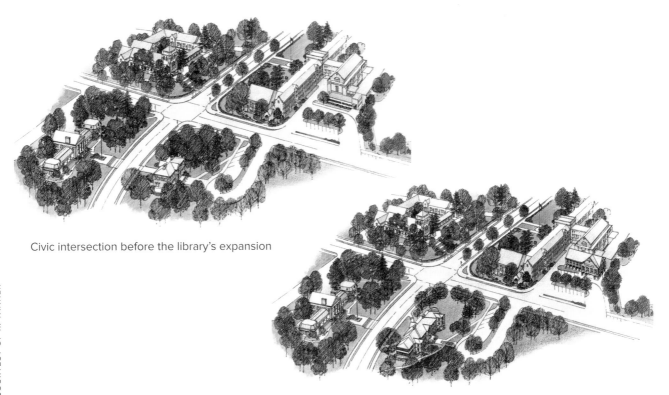

Civic intersection before the library's expansion

Civic intersection after the library's expansion

Design Objectives

The building committee worked with the architects to establish the following design objectives, which emerged over time:

- Provide seamless connections to the past; emulate the detail and finishes of the original Georgian building.
- Make the building code-compliant, handicapped-accessible, and energy-efficient.
- Intersperse reading spaces within the book collections.
- Enhance the visibility and continuity of the art gallery.
- Create a more interconnected series of spaces.
- Establish varied pathways of movement through the library.

New Plan

The building committee reviewed the three expansion schemes and chose the 8,000 to 10,000-square-foot option, which proposed three-level additions at each end of the building; this arrangement was inspired by the grand houses designed by Charles Platt (1861–1933), a distinguished architect of neoclassical residences. With the addition of the two new wings, the Bronxville Library would become a 20,650-square-foot building.

The expanded building functions with a bilaterally symmetrical central hall plan flanked by less formal wings. The building balances the scale of the elongated mass of the Village Hall, which is located across Pondfield Road, directly on axis with the library entry. In the expanded wing to the north is a

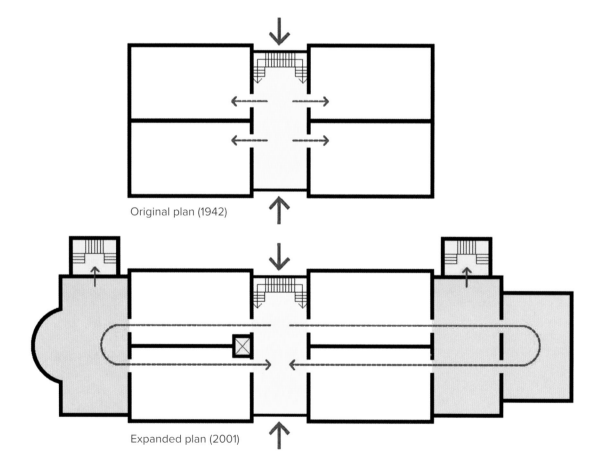

Original plan (1942)

Expanded plan (2001)

Expansion Concept

Orginal Center Hall / Stair   New Stairs and Elevator   New Additions new bow window, which overlooks the green space at the four corners. The new community room is located at the lowest level of the new south addition; it has terraced seating with good sight lines and easy access for the handicapped.

A new idea emerged for the art gallery. Moving the library director's office to the north on the second floor opened the center hall and doubled the space for a gallery to house the permanent collection. The center hall areas on the first floor and also at the lower level provide additional gallery space. This three-level display of art places an important function at the center of the building.

Another dramatic change in the building is the addition of two new code-required staircases at the north and south ends. These fire exit staircases make movement within the building easier and more convenient. Library users no longer have to return to the center hall grand stair whenever they want to reach other levels. Within the formal setting of the building, the library has become functionally less formal and more serendipitous. Throughout the building, the neoclassical detailing is preserved, emulated, and enhanced, maintaining the aura of a gracious, comfortable house with an inspiring art collection.

Green Initiatives

The Bronxville Library was designed in an era when buildings were constructed with single-pane glass windows and little or no insulation in the walls or roof. The following changes improved the energy efficiency of the building:

- New double-glazed wood windows in both new wings and throughout the original building.
- An efficient heating and cooling system with fan coils that allow for comfort adjustments in separate areas within the building.
- Well-insulated walls and roofs in the new wings.
- Insulation in the attic of the original building.

Bronxville Library after restoration and expansion. Inset: Original Bronxville Library.

Second-floor gallery, expanded and transformed

Original second-floor gallery space

Restored window and stair details

Collaborative Strategies

Collaborative efforts in the design, construction, and furnishings of the building were successful.

- The building committee included the five-member library board of directors and members of the professional staff. All of the committee members were vocal, articulate, and committed to providing the community with an exceptional building.
- The committee, in collaboration with the architect, established clear objectives.
- The three alternative building sizes and layouts were carefully evaluated.
- Building committee meetings were held twice a month and were increased to weekly meetings during construction. The library board president visited the construction site nearly every day.
- An active subcommittee selected finishes, furnishings, fabrics, colors, and Oriental carpets. The members explored antique shops and consignment stores, searching for mahogany and cherry tables and chairs that would be appropriate in the new reading spaces of the library. They found vintage brass floor lamps and cut-glass table lamps to harmonize with the dark wood furnishings.

Achieving Success: The Transformation of a Grand House

The Bronxville Library was originally designed to resemble a grand house to celebrate books, paintings, tranquility, and the comfort of gracious interior spaces. The new plan added seven rooms to the original ten and transformed major areas: the space for children is twice the size; the central art gallery at the second level is twice as large, and the building itself is two times its original size. While the concept of separate rooms has been maintained, they are connected in a fashion that allows more public patterns of movement. The building continues to be the Bronxville Library from 1942, but it has become a larger community cultural center with twenty-first-century amenities.

New reading porch on the south side of the library

The bay window in the new north wing overlooks the village's main civic intersection

The Impact

Librarian Involvement in the Design Process Benefits Patrons and Staff

By **PAT ROOT, TESSYMOL JOHN, AND MARIANNE WINGERTZAHN**

THE ORIGINAL BRONXVILLE PUBLIC LIBRARY WAS small and had not changed substantially since it was constructed in 1942. As a result of the extensive transformation and expansion, it is difficult to pinpoint a single best feature of the new library. Overall, the most noteworthy result of the project is simply having more space, and particularly space that our patrons and community have used so actively since the building reopened.

One of the most successful elements of the new space is the attractive and functional new community room on the lower level. Stepped seating, good sight lines, and handicapped accessibility throughout the room enhance the viewing experience for audiences. In addition, the lower-level space is used as an art gallery for special exhibitions; the

permanent collection is housed on the upper floors. There is an adjacent studio for recording programs and meetings to be broadcast on a local television channel.

The community room is booked nearly every day for library programming (films, concerts, lectures, drama) or by local organizations (programs, events, meetings). This new space replaces our old meeting room, which was small, tired, and rarely used. Adjacent to the community room, we now have a new meeting room that is ideal for quieter purposes, such as meditation, adult coloring classes, tutoring, and book clubs.

On the first floor, each of two paneled reading rooms contains a fireplace, antique furniture, Oriental carpets, and selections from the library's fine

The young adults space on the second floor extends into the north-facing addition.

The children's library on the second floor has a spacious storytime area at the south-facing reading porch.

art collection—all of which were central features of the original building. These cherished rooms remain popular with readers. Our patrons also love the two new reading rooms located at each end of the building. Oversized windows fill the areas with natural light and offer tranquil views of the library's tree-filled green.

The new teen room, to the right (north) of the central stair on the second floor, offers a dedicated space for gatherings and age-related programming. To the left (south) of the central stair is the storytime/crafts/multipurpose space that was added to the children's library. All of these spaces are heavily used and allow for more activities than ever before.

One of the satisfying results of the expanded and renovated building is that, like the old library, it is still an attractive, comfortable space that seems like a private house filled with art and antiques. This is

DESIGN TEAM
Peter Gisolfi
Michael Tribe
Klaus Kalmbach
Crosby Scott
Diane Collins
Christopher Wadsworth
Joseph Keating

PHOTOGRAPHY BY
Norman McGrath
Robert Mintzes

particularly notable at the top of the grand staircase on the second floor, where space previously assigned to offices has been transformed into a central art gallery that overlooks the library's lawn. Patrons constantly compliment us on the beauty of our library.

The enlarged building has greatly improved the efficiency of our staff.

With the additional space, we are able to organize our book collection more logically, and to assign other library materials to designated areas. For example, we now have a dedicated fiction room, which includes stacks and a bright, comfortable reading space. Two major changes are particularly beneficial to librarians: before the library was accessible to the handicapped, we had to carry books out to the curb to serve these patrons. Now, with a sloping lawn and a gentle path to the front door, which operates at the press of a button, all of

The new community room was created from unexcavated basement space.

our patrons are able to come inside. The original building had no elevator, so to retrieve books from the lower level and the second floor, we had to carry volumes up and down a narrow, metal staircase or use a manual dumbwaiter. Our hands would burn from pulling on the ropes of the book-filled dumbwaiter as we lifted and lowered it.

With no staff workroom in the original building, we made do in scattered places throughout the building. For example, four of us had desks crammed into the staff kitchenette. We had to bring new books upstairs to process them, and then carry them back down to put them into circulation. The new first-floor workroom, located just behind the elevator and circulation desk, contains generous counter space and computer workstations. Now, we can sort and process books and other library materials more quickly and efficiently in this well-appointed and properly located space.

Recommendations for Librarians during Design and Construction

- Visit other libraries. Note which ideas work and which do not; communicate these observations to the design team during the planning and design phases.
- Include the library's professional staff and solicit their opinions as plans develop.

A new art gallery leads to the community room.

- Encourage the staff to tour the site during construction in order to get a feel for how the new spaces will function.
- Don't be shy about asking for guidance in reading plans and drawings. For instance, we did not realize that our reference desk would be placed in the center of the reference/computer room. We changed the location so we could view the entire space and its occupants at a glance.
- In order to minimize noise in the adult spaces, locate the children's room on the main floor. (We were unable to relocate our second-floor children's room because our first floor is devoted to historically valuable rooms that could not change function.)
- Similarly, locate the teen room with other high-traffic activities.
- If your building will be closed to the public during construction, take advantage of the temporary location to attract new patrons, become more familiar with the interlibrary loan system, and develop new ways to serve the public.
- To smooth the transition to the new space, delay the opening of the building until all the books are organized on shelves and the furniture and other library accoutrements are in place.
- Approach the project as an opportunity to learn and focus on the positive aspects of change. Because our director and board kept us informed and involved throughout, we can look back positively on the entire process.

Pat Root was a reference librarian at the Bronxville Public Library from 1988 to 2016.

Tessymol John has been a reference librarian at the Bronxville Public Library since 2001.

Marianne Wingertzahn has been head of circulation at the Bronxville Public Library since 1986.

Dobbs Ferry Public Library
Dobbs Ferry, New York

chapter 4

The Planning Process

An Active Library Emerges from a Unique Village Site

By JULIE LOWY

THE VILLAGE OF DOBBS FERRY, NEW YORK, WAS SETTLED IN 1873 AND NAMED for Jeremiah Dobbs, a fisherman, who supplemented his income by taking advantage of the village's riverfront location to run a ferry service across the Hudson River.

The original library in Dobbs Ferry opened in 1909 in a two-story building that had been constructed before the turn of the century, possibly at the same time that Jeremiah Dobbs was traversing the Hudson. The library, located at the intersection of Main and Cedar streets, served the village's needs for nearly 100 years. But age had taken its toll, and in the 1990s the mayor recognized the need for change.

Engineers hired by the village had evaluated the building and determined that it could collapse under the weight of the book collection. New supporting beams, installed as a safety measure, obstructed public access through the dark, narrow walkways. The building was not only deteriorating and hazardous, but it was not accessible to the handicapped, it contained only one small bathroom, it did not accommodate current technology, and it lacked a community room and adequate seating for patrons. This building would have to close.

Moving Quickly

But if the building closed, village residents would be denied access to the Westchester Library System (WLS). They would be unable to obtain a library card for use in another WLS library, and without a library card, they could not take advantage of any WLS services. In short, the building was too small, out of date, hazardous, code-deficient, and could deny the reading public access to a library.

The library board moved quickly to explore options: should they rehabilitate the current building, or instead construct a new library? The board interviewed six architects. In their deliberations, the board members considered each architect's approach to library design, their availability to begin work promptly, and their willingness to collaborate with a diverse board whose members sometimes held opposing points of view. When Peter Gisolfi talked about resolving opposing views through collaboration, we felt he was addressing our situation directly. With the architect in place, a building committee was organized.

Project Requirements and Site Selection

The building committee was made up of two library board members, a village trustee, the library director, and the architects. After careful deliberations, the committee developed a list of requirements for the project:

- Design a building compatible with the character of the village.
- Connect the library to the Hudson River, with water views throughout.
- Meet current building codes, including ADA accessibility.
- Locate the community room, exhibition space, and a conference room on street level, for daytime and after-hours use.
- Include a periodicals room overlooking the Hudson River, and an outdoor reading terrace.
- Create a separate children's library with a storytelling space.
- Create a quiet library on the second level for the adult collections and seating.
- Include current computer technology and plan for future flexibility.
- Provide parking for staff.

The new community room was created from unexcavated basement space.

Once the requirements were established, the building committee and the architects explored whether the existing building could be transformed in place and expanded onto a small neighboring site. This plan was vetoed. Transforming and expanding the building would be difficult and costly, and the neighbors objected to demolishing the shoe repair shop and the apartment above it on the adjacent property.

The village decided to move forward with new construction. Several sites were evaluated:

- The Gateway at the junction of Route 9 and Ashford Avenue was a major intersection on a state road. Developing part of that site would require an oil cleanup, state approval, and an outlay of $5 million for the property.
- Taking advantage of property already owned by the village presented clear advantages: no competition with developers to purchase the property, cost efficiency, and the ability to speed up the process by eliminating village approval to make a purchase.
- Village-owned properties included the site of a steep cliff on Cedar Street, an adjacent building in poor condition, and a small village parking lot on Main Street. Ultimately, the library board and village trustees determined that the parking lot, situated below street level at 55 Main Street, would meet the requirements.

Involving the Community

The building committee recognized the need for a new library and, considering the condition of the existing building, appreciated the speed with which the process had to begin. However, convincing the public proved challenging. Some residents questioned whether a new library was truly needed; others failed to understand the code compliance issues, and still others needed to be convinced that without a working library, New York State law would rule out nearby library services. A major challenge came from a vocal minority that objected to losing the parking lot. Still others wanted to use the library project to resolve current planning issues in the village, such as the transformation of the Gateway.

The building committee, with the help of the architects, embarked on a plan to involve the public in the proposed library project. A professional fund-raiser suggested asking for significant donations from wealthy individuals, but this idea was quickly rejected as too high-powered an approach for the relaxed environment of the village. A local graphic artist designed a brochure describing how an updated, modern library would benefit village residents. The brochure also outlined various fund-raising categories, such as buying a brick, a bench, or a bookshelf, for example. These measures helped generate community support, but amounted to relatively small contributions.

A surprise bequest solidified the viability of the project. In her will, Doris Volland listed the new Dobbs Ferry Public Library as an heir to $2.2 million from her estate—half for the building itself, and half for future capital improvements. The rest of the building cost was paid for by a public bond. Groundbreaking took place in September 2001.

A Successful Library Project

The new library is a success in many ways:

- Circulation of the collection and community use of the library have increased significantly.
- The flexible community room meets the need for various functions.
- The outdoor reading terrace is a welcoming space with spectacular river views.
- The children's library is an inviting space for storytelling.
- The exhibitions space, near the community room, features the work of local artists, photographers, and schoolchildren.

- The community room provides outstanding acoustics for musical performances.
- The library is equipped with present-day technology and offers computers for public use.

Those of us who served on the building committee and the various subcommittees dealing with furnishings, supplies, and so on, learned a great deal about undertaking a civic project. We saw first-hand that through the process of serious collaboration, essential public buildings are proposed, constructed, and can ultimately overcome challenges to become accepted and valued additions to the community. Such was the case with the new Dobbs Ferry Public Library.

Suggestions

We offer these suggestions to community leaders who are in the throes of evaluating new or expanded libraries:

- Hire an owner's representative who can manage the construction. We did not have an owner's representative. The village manager and the architects had to share some of that responsibility.
- The architects for the Dobbs Ferry Public Library were effective in describing the project to the public. Be sure you hire an architect who can present well.
- Insist on frequent communication between the public and the design professionals involved in the project.
- We recommend a small building committee, whose members are passionately involved in every aspect of the project.

Julie Lowy was a member of the library board from 1996 to 2000, and was president in 2002.

Children's Library

Circulation desk and periodicals room beyond

Dobbs Ferry Library looking east from the Hudson River

The Design

Two Settings Present an Architectural Challenge

By **PETER GISOLFI**

THE PUBLIC LIBRARY IN DOBBS FERRY, NEW YORK, occupies two settings—the smaller setting is a picturesque, riverfront village in Westchester County, New York; the second setting is a hillside location within the larger landscape of the Hudson River Valley with views of the water.

The village center is made up of densely packed, rectangular buildings that come right to the edge of the sidewalk and create a series of defined streets that slope and wind. On the lower end of Main Street, at a bend in the roadway, was a small parking lot. After investigating two other possibilities, this piece of land—a compact site with a clear view of the Hudson River—was chosen for a new library. The architectural challenge was to design a library consistent with the fabric of the village, while creating an important civic building that took advan-

View of the library looking west to the Hudson River

tage of the river view. The design of the building reflects our understanding of these two settings.

Program Requirements

The building committee included two members of the library board of trustees, a village trustee, the library director, and the architects. The members established the following requirements:

- Design and construct a new library to serve a village of approximately 11,000 people.
- Evaluate three potential sites for the library.
- Once the Main Street location had been selected, the architects were asked to design a building to take advantage of the river view.
- Reuse some of the existing parking at the lower level for staff.
- Locate the most active public spaces—the children's library, periodicals, the circulation desk, and the community room—at the first-floor level.
- Locate the quieter adult areas on the second level.

Design Objectives

The building committee established the following design objectives:

- Relate the building to the scale and fabric of the village.
- Embrace the Hudson River Valley.
- Provide transparency between the various functions of the library.
- Design the building to be easily managed by a small staff.
- Create a community cultural center.

New Plan

The new building was conceived as two rectangular wings, each parallel to its neighbor. These two rectangular forms, with their distinctive gable roofs, are connected by a flat-roofed, single-story entry pavilion. The two wings and the curving edge of Main Street define an exterior courtyard at the library's entrance. Like many neighboring buildings, the library is constructed of red brick, and

Dobbs Ferry Library in its village context on Main Street

it has a clock tower that rises above the roof and emulates the towers on other civic buildings in the village center.

The larger wing, two stories high, contains the community auditorium, public restrooms, confer-

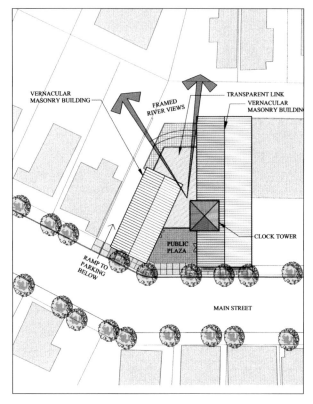

Site concept plan

ence room, recent acquisitions, and the circulation desk on the first floor; the adult areas and reference room are located on the second floor. The smaller, one-story wing contains the children's library. The center section houses periodicals and also provides access to the outdoor reading terrace. At the lower level are mechanical space and parking. Overall, this configuration puts the most active spaces at grade, and locates the quieter, more contemplative spaces on the second floor. Patrons can view the Hudson River from the entry pavilion, the outdoor reading terrace, the conference room and staff offices, and the second-floor adult library. The library's clock tower is visible from the river.

Within the larger wing, the first and second levels are visually connected by an opening in the first floor's ceiling, which is accented by a skylight in the gable roof above. With this open connection, the library can be operated with a staff of only three people—one at the circulation desk, another in the children's library, and a third upstairs in the adult area. The building is transparent externally and internally. The entry pavilion is entirely made of glass, which allows for transparency to the street and transparency to the river view. The separate wings are internally open to the entry pavilion.

Green Initiatives

The green initiatives for the Dobbs Ferry Public Library followed good practice of the time:

- The walls and roofs are well-insulated.
- The windows are double-glazed.
- The mechanical system is energy efficient.
- Photovoltaic panels to generate electricity are located on the south-facing portions of the gable roofs.

Collaborative Strategies

- The board members of the building committee acted as the primary client for the project.
- The building committee reviewed analytical drawings for three potential sites; it was a lengthy process. The selected site had two main advantages: it had the best river view, and it was owned by the village.
- Meetings were held weekly and every aspect of the design was discussed in detail.
- The collaborative process for designing the library was complicated. Decision making ultimately succeeded because the design objectives were understood and accepted and served as the basis for the many smaller design decisions that were required.

Achieving Success

When the construction was complete, the library moved from its 7,500-square-foot quarters to the new building of 16,000 square feet. The library relates to its settings on Main Street and on the hillside that overlooks the Hudson River. It is well adapted to the scale of the village, it emulates precedents established by other civic buildings, and it creates a welcoming courtyard on Main Street. The internal transparency and simplicity of the layout allow the library to be operated efficiently.

The Dobbs Ferry Public Library joins people and place. Its distinctive presence draws in visitors and invites them to connect visually to the urban streetscape of the village and the wider landscape of the Hudson River Valley. It offers a broad range of library services and activities, including recitals, lectures, book talks, exhibits, exercise classes, children's programs, and teen events. It is an active place and an asset for the community.

Courtyard at the entry to the new library

The Impact

New Library Offers Expansive Interiors and River Views

By **EDWARD CANORA**

THE ORIGINAL DOBBS FERRY PUBLIC LIBRARY WAS so cramped and overcrowded that two people could not pass between the rows of shelving without bumping into each other. The children's area was located at the top of a narrow, unsafe staircase. The area around the circulation desk was also a safety concern; it was situated so that patrons could walk up behind the staff without being seen or heard. And most concerning, the building was in danger of collapse due to the weight of the book collection.

The village trustees considered alternatives, but ultimately determined that even a renovated building was too small to serve the growing population of the village of Dobbs Ferry. After a prolonged search for a new site, the board of trustees granted approval to construct a new library on a municipal parking lot close to the library's original home.

The new building, with its distinctive clock tower, is more than twice the size of the old library and provides amenities that were lacking in the old building. The new building has a separate children's room, away from quiet study areas; it has a community room/art gallery for lectures and performances; a conference room is used by the library administration and local community groups; and an adult reading room and reading terrace offer quiet getaways for patrons, plus scenic views of the Hudson River.

New Library Doubles the Size

The new space is open and expansive—16,000 square feet on two floors. When entering the library, patrons encounter the circulation desk and are greeted by a friendly staff in a bright and airy space. The circulation area is accessible to patrons but is semi-enclosed for the security of the staff. Patrons can browse the collection unimpeded. The children's room, on the main floor, includes a small storytelling alcove and shelves scaled for young people. Popular with our youngsters is a summer reading game displayed on the walls showing how the children are progressing as they read their way to prizes.

The Dobbs Ferry Public Library is an active place that reflects the public's belief that a strong library contributes to a strong community. The library's community room displays the work of local artists, photographers, and students. A smaller conference room is available for meetings and small gatherings. Throughout the library are reading spaces with comfortable seating, as well as workspaces furnished with large tables.

One of the drawbacks of the old library was restricted movement for patrons as well as staff. Now, openness best describes the new space. Patrons can browse individually or together with a friend, and staff can circulate throughout the building, helping patrons find books and materials, and pointing out collections that appeal to special interests.

When thinking about the library in Dobbs Ferry, the view comes to mind. Looking west from the reading terrace and from multiple locations within the library are breathtaking views of the Hudson River. The design of the library takes full advantage of the village's proximity to the river and its ever-changing moods—quiet and serene on some days, while powerful and ferocious on others. The river is often the inspiration for reading choices and narrative themes.

Recommendations for Success

Undertaking a design and construction project, whether for a new library building or the alteration of an existing one, is a daunting task that requires various constituencies—librarians, patrons, administrators, trustees, architects and interior designers, contractors, and taxpayers—to work together and collaborate thoughtfully in order to arrive at an outcome beneficial to all. Based on my experiences and observations during the design and construction of the new Dobbs Ferry Public Library building, I offer the following recommendations:

- Stay informed and be involved, even if you are not serving on a committee.
- Visit other libraries to evaluate good features as well as those that don't work well.
- Encourage staff tours throughout the design and construction phases; solicit staff opinions and make them part of the plan.
- Don't be shy. Ask questions and ask for explanations if plans are unclear.
- Be sure to separate quiet adult spaces from noisy children's areas.
- Include a space for teens and locate it in a high-traffic area to contain noise.
- If the library must close during construction, consider operating from a nearby storefront.
- For a smooth transition, make sure that all materials are properly shelved prior to reopening.
- Enjoy the process. Don't be discouraged if setbacks arise. Keep looking forward and you will be rewarded by staff and patrons who appreciate their new surroundings.

DESIGN TEAM
Frank Craine
Peter Gisolfi
Garth McIntosh

PHOTOGRAPHY BY
Norman McGrath
Robert Mintzes

Edward Canora has been a member of the Dobbs Ferry Public Library staff since 1999. He is a librarian who currently serves as business manager and technical services supervisor.

Reading room overlooking the Hudson River

Reading room detail

Dobbs Ferry Public Library in its village context

The Planning Process

A Small Branch Library Expands to Meet the Needs of Its Patrons

By JANE MARSH

THE BYRAM SHUBERT LIBRARY, ONE OF TWO BRANCHES IN THE GREENWICH (Connecticut) Library System, was a 5,000-square-foot building that had opened in 1974. Primarily, it served a community district of three elementary schools with a total of about 800 students. Based on the goals of the main library's strategic plan, the branch libraries played an important role in their neighborhoods:

- They offered a current collection of reading and reference materials and also provided access to the broader collection and services at the main library.
- They served as community centers, attracting patrons to diverse educational and cultural programs.

By 2004, the student population in the three elementary schools in the district had increased to nearly 1,000 students, with a total population of more than 8,300 people in the area surrounding the library. Many residents used the library for the usual services as well as social interaction.

It became clear that the Byram Shubert Library, with its limited size and unusual one-large-room configuration, could not adequately serve its expanding and increasingly diverse population. The goal of the expansion was to offer superior library services, to serve the cultural and intellectual interests of its constituency, and to be a responsive leader in a rapidly changing environment; programming had to expand to serve a multiethnic Spanish-speaking and Portuguese-speaking community.

The old library building did not have the space to serve the range of patrons who visited daily—to browse, read books, use the computers, socialize, and attend classes and programs. Display and reading space was limited, and there was no quiet space for adults to relax while activities were going on in other parts of the library. Computers were in constant demand, and space was needed to add more computer stations, and expand the CD and DVD collections, the teen collection, and, particularly, Spanish-language books. The furnishings and lighting were limited and outdated, and the spaces for small group meetings and conversations in English and Spanish were inadequate.

Evolution of the Planning Process

When presented with the proposal to consider expansion of the Byram Shubert Library, the board of trustees approved a plan to justify the project. A steering committee comprised of current and former trustees, community leaders, and individuals with building expertise met regularly for more than

a year; in that time, they developed a proposal to explore the need for expansion, defined the goals of a larger building, and set an agenda for moving forward.

The trustees approved the concept and allocated funds for a consultant to develop a space-needs assessment and building program. The trustees defined the criteria for a library consulting firm, interviewed several potential candidates, and in 2004 selected Library Development Solutions (LDS) to conduct the space needs assessment and develop a building program. At this point, a collaborative effort between the steering committee and LDS included the following:

- Community surveys and interviews
- Focus groups
- Open town meetings

View of the Byram Shubert Library, with the original building to the left and the new addition to the right

- Staff interviews
- Census tract analysis for potential funding

Throughout this process, status reports were reviewed monthly at the trustees' meetings. A comprehensive fund-raising plan was developed and key potential contributors were approached to determine their support and interest. LDS presented its findings to the trustees of the Greenwich Library, which approved the plan to move forward with the project.

Once approval for the project was obtained, the steering committee researched, analyzed, and selected the architectural firm that would lead the design and development stages. The steering committee (renamed the building committee) visited several libraries in the tri-state area as part of the due diligence process.

The building committee conducted a thorough and competitive review of more than a dozen prospective architectural firms; three finalists were selected to present their credentials and vision for the new Byram Shubert Library. The committee unanimously selected Peter Gisolfi Associates. The firm's critical thinking and respect for existing buildings was evident to all.

Throughout the process, the Gisolfi team presented concepts and diagrams that were considered and vetted by the trustees. In addition, the library director met with Greenwich officials to keep them apprised of progress; the town of Greenwich provides about 75 percent of the library's operating budget. One caveat posed by the town was that no additional staff members would need to be hired to operate the expanded library.

The project was a true public/private partnership in that funds came from the private sector, the town of Greenwich, a State of Connecticut State Library Grant, and a federally funded Community Development Block Grant. The newly expanded library opened in 2008, approximately six years after the project was initiated.

Advice for Board Members Preparing to Build or Rebuild

- Define goals early in the process.
- Validate the need for the expansion/renovation before seeking board support.
- Develop a support team able to objectively assess a need to proceed with the project.
- Reach out to others with the expertise and knowledge to offer advice on the needs assessment plan.
- Identify sources of funding—private, local, state, and federal.
- Hire a well-qualified project manager and coordinate regularly with him or her.
- Develop a comprehensive communications plan to provide regular project updates to the local community, including patrons, staff members, donors and potential donors, town administrators, and board members.

The overall process involved completing a library expansion and transformation that exceeded our expectations. Common purpose, open communications, motivated library staff, dedicated volunteers, and skilled architects and builders contributed to this success.

Jane Marsh served as former chairman of the steering committee of the Byram Shubert Library and was a trustee of the Greenwich Library from 2001 to 2008 and from 2009 to 2016.

The Design

In the New Library, Children and Adults Work Harmoniously

By **PETER GISOLFI**

THE BYRAM SHUBERT LIBRARY IS LOCATED IN THE Byram neighborhood within the town of Greenwich in southeastern Connecticut. The original library was a 1974 cruciform building that was essentially one large room accented by a central skylight. The building was set on a small site, surrounded by parking. An elementary school is situated nearby.

Because of the library's proximity to the school, many of the students come to the library at the end of the school day. Many of their parents also meet at the library to pick up their children and socialize with other parents. Because of the one-room configuration of the original library, it became so noisy in the afternoons that most adult patrons, who were unconnected to the school community, would leave the building. Clearly, Byram's population was inadequately served by the size and layout of the library.

Program Requirements

The town of Greenwich established a steering committee to define the improvements that needed to be made in order to better meet the needs of Byram's residents. That committee of former and current library trustees and community members became the building committee for the project. That committee, in collaboration with the architects, established the following program requirements:

- Double the size of the library from 5,500 to 11,000 square feet.
- Add a generously sized children's room that is

physically and acoustically separated from the adult areas.

- Add a new community room that can function separately from the rest of the library.
- Enhance computer technology throughout the building.
- Create a more rational parking plan for the site that allows students to walk safely to and from the elementary school.

Design Objectives

Once the program requirements had been established, the building committee and the architects identified the design objectives for the project:

- Create a transformed and expanded library that allows different age groups to inhabit

the building at the same time.
- Configure the expanded library so that the current staff would be able to operate it.
- Respect and enhance the architectural language of the original design.
- Design a building that is more energy efficient.
- Create a site plan that is better adapted to the setting.

Alternative Concepts

The architects developed six diagrammatic solutions and presented them to the building committee. Each scheme was evaluated collaboratively to determine which one would best serve the objectives that had been established.

New children's library

Schemes 1A, 1B, and 1C featured an addition on the north side of the building and included both one-story and two-story solutions. Schemes 2A, 2B, and 2C placed the addition on the east side and, again, looked at both one-story and two-story designs.

A two-level scheme was chosen; it faces east with a view to the playing field. This solution also features less paving on the east side, which allows for better views of the green space. The selected scheme serves the requirements of separated functions and responds to the existing site.

New Plan

The library, with a new two-story structure adjacent to the original building, has been transformed in terms of its setting and function. The new addition of approximately 5,500 square feet creates a split-level connection to the original library, with the community room below the main level and the children's room above it. This configuration successfully separates the intensively used children's area on the upper level from the quieter adult space one-half level below. The configuration of the adult library space on the main level offers differentiated zones for privacy, research, and browsing. Computer technology is enhanced throughout the library, and more workstations are available to meet user demand.

The 1974 library was a symmetrical space with the main entrance on an axis with the central skylight. In the new arrangement, the entrance is at the junction of the older building and the new addi-

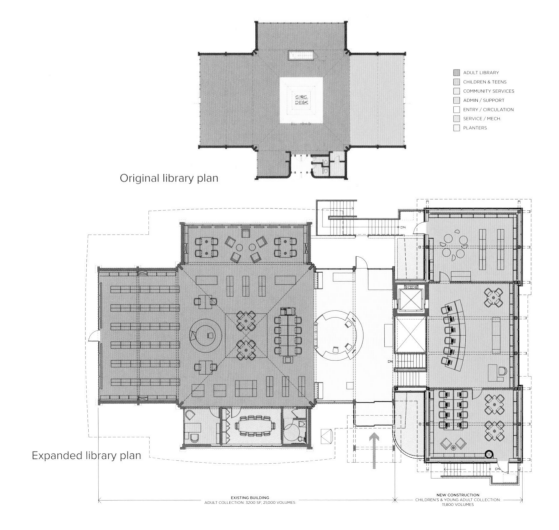

Original library plan

Expanded library plan

tion, creating an informal and more logical circulation pattern. At the entry, one can immediately see the adult library on the left and the up-and-down stairways on the right; there is also an elevator that connects to all three levels.

The addition imitates the architectural language of the original building, with its undulating roof forms, exposed wood glulam (glued and laminated) beams, and acoustical wood ceilings. The glulam beams and wood ceilings in the older building were refinished and lightened to closely match the new wood in the addition. Exterior brick and trim colors unite the original building and the new addition. The new space maintains and enhances the spirit of the original.

Green Initiatives

The design of the building effectively reduces operating and maintenance costs in the following ways:

- It uses a new, more efficient mechanical system.
- Large expanses of double-glazed walls and clerestory windows flood the interior of the new wing with daylight.

- Energy-efficient lighting and multilevel controls are used throughout the building.
- The building uses efficient insulation, and natural materials and finishes throughout.
- The redesigned site has less impervious surface area and more green spaces with no loss of on-site parking. Traffic flow and pedestrian circulation are improved.

Collaborative Strategies

Six design solutions for the library were offered to the building committee. By examining, analyzing, and critiquing each scheme, the committee members became active participants in the design of the library.

Achieving Success

The community has embraced the transformed library, as evidenced by the increase in patronage. The library is still a popular destination for young children, and now it is a place where children and adults simultaneously enjoy the welcoming environment.

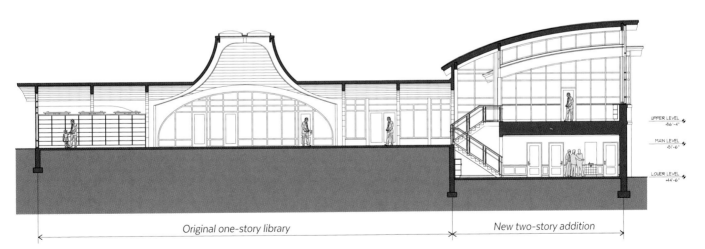

UPPER LEVEL
+56'-4"

MAIN LEVEL
+51'-6"

LOWER LEVEL
+44'-6"

Original one-story library   *New two-story addition*

Section through the expanded library

View of the transformed library from the new circulation desk

The Impact

Let There Be Light, Let There Be Space

By **MIGUEL GARCIA-COLON**

AS I APPROACH THE BYRAM SHUBERT LIBRARY every morning on my way to work, I see a building where form and function are in harmony, where beauty and workability coincide. This is a building that was designed to delight its staff and patrons, and to accommodate the constant activity that occurs inside.

Sometime in the 1930s, library services were first offered in Byram—at several locations. In 1974 a permanent site was chosen and a dedicated library building was constructed right in the center of a residential area, where the neighbors could easily walk to the library from their homes.

The 1974 building was the result of financial support from the Shubert and Jennings families. Our new library now houses 37,000 items and has expanded from a single space of 5,000 square feet on one level to 10,000 square feet on three levels.

I remember my concern in the old library that adults would flee the building when the public school day was over, because the children from the nearby elementary school would rush across the street and pour into the building with high-spirited exuberance. To compound the problem, the children's and adult collections were integrated, and only four computers were available in that same small shared space.

Now, of course, thanks to the expansion and transformation of the library, the children have their own space, adults have theirs, and teens have a place separate from the other two—all coexisting harmoniously within the building.

Transitioning from the Old to the New

Patrons and staff alike faced the prospect of construction with mixed feelings. Yes, everyone wanted more space and the other amenities that the redesign promised. But patrons worried about being without the library services they had depended on for so many years; and the staff wondered if they would be able to serve patrons responsively.

69

Happily, we found rental space in the lower level of a church building across the street from the library, and we operated from there while the library building was in the throes of expansion. Although the space did not allow for a full collection and all services, we were able at least to offer a core collection and recent acquisitions, and we could serve the public reasonably well in our temporary quarters. In essence, we operated as a storefront library, and were even able to offer programs within the building. The important facts are that we kept the library open, we operated nearby, and we served the public.

As another positive aspect of the transition, we found this time of moving and storage to be a great opportunity to weed the entire collection, and to discard old furniture to make way for new furnishings that were custom-made for the library. As it turned out, the staff was extremely busy and productive during the construction period.

Features of the New Library

It is unfair to single out one or two features of our library as the best ones. For instance, unlike the relatively dark interior of the 1974 building, the expanded library has large windows for bright, daylit spaces that bring the outside in. The atmosphere is always cheerful and uplifting for patrons and staff alike. Other items on our patrons' best features list are the new magazine and newspaper area

View from the children's library to the new entry

and the enhanced technology spaces, which offer many computers available for all ages to access in separate locations. There is no more waiting for a workstation to open up.

The library staff finds that the separate areas for adults, teens, and children, each with appropriate collections, make it easier to maintain, evaluate, and update the books and related materials. The spaces themselves are open and flexible, permitting various arrangements to best serve a planned or serendipitous activity. The staff also likes the more central location of the combined circulation/reference/information desk, where the old and new buildings join. From this vantage point, without adding staff, we are able to observe the activity on three levels throughout the building, and we can also greet patrons as they enter the library, setting a welcoming tone for visitors.

From my experience, I offer this advice:

- Do not close the library; operate out of temporary space to keep people coming to the library, and to maintain the momentum.
- Weed the collection thoroughly.
- To avoid confusion, do not rush to open before everything is in place. The public has been patient for a long time; you want them to feel that any inconveniences were worth the wait.
- Invite people to visit the new library. The new features offered in a larger, modernized library will attract new patrons.

How the New Space Impacts Day-to-Day Life in the Library

Since the opening, the expanded library has been transformational. All of the library services are offered, and we can serve all of our populations at the same time. These are enormous pluses for staff as well as patrons, who are constantly telling us how fortunate they are to have this facility right in the midst of their community. Overall, the library has added to the quality of life in the neighborhood and has increased property values.

With its distinct spaces for programming, the library is able to increase its outreach to the community. The multipurpose program room can seat 125 people for lectures, musicals, and dramatic performances, and can also serve as an art gallery. The conference room is available for 16 to 18 people and was cleverly created from the original entryway in the older building. The children's library is spacious enough to accommodate about 30 parents and youngsters for storytimes and programs of special interest. Remarkably, all three programming spaces can be in operation at the same time, with no interference from each other.

The library offers the pleasures of light, spaciousness, responsive service, and an extensive collection—all in an atmosphere of warmth and beauty. Even the site now contributes to tranquility: the conference room overlooks a flower garden; from their room, the children can see a park; and from the periodicals area, readers can look up to the sight of majestic trees. For me, working in this handsome building is inspiring. I love coming to work every day.

Our library has changed in significant ways:

- The new library serves multiple age groups simultaneously.
- The communal gathering areas provide opportunities for more programming.
- The reference and study areas are furnished with new, custom-designed worktables, and the reading areas offer upholstered seating on the main and lower levels.
- Daylight and transparency bring a sense of unexpected joy to the building and its users.
- Site plan improvements provide pleasant views from generous windows and allow students from the nearby elementary school safe passage as they walk (or run) to the library.
- The new library provides ample space for browsing—with a

Quiet seating area in the new addition

special area for new acquisitions—as well as a variety of meeting spaces where the community can gather.

Contributions Librarians Can Make to the Design of Library Buildings

- Having worked in the original library, the staff is familiar with the building's virtues as well as its shortcomings. Librarians should participate freely and with a strong voice in the design process.
- The staff should visit other libraries to see what works well, and what to avoid in the new library.
- Librarians should constantly monitor the design process so that the new library will operate effortlessly for patrons and staff alike.
- Librarians should articulate the aspirations of the library users and staff.
- The rapport that developed between the librarians and the architects should continue after the new building opens. In that way, the librarians and architects can comfortably collaborate on future adjustments to the plan.

Of the many design elements incorporated into a new building, perhaps none are as beneficial to librarians and patrons as daylight and spaciousness. Let there be light, and let there be space.

Miguel Garcia-Colon is manager of the Byram Shubert branch of the Greenwich Library.

DESIGN TEAM
Michael Tribe
Klaus Kalmbach
Patricia Montero
Joori Suh
Julien Alexis
Michelle Benitez-Ortiz

PHOTOGRAPHY BY
Robert Mintzes
Philip Tribe

PART II

Academic and School Libraries

The Planning Process

Thinking Big Produces a Positive Result

By **PHILIP VARIANO**

O N AUGUST 4, 2007, A VIOLENT THUNDERSTORM SWEPT THROUGH WEST-chester County, New York. According to weather reports, 375 lightning strikes occurred within a five-mile radius of Tarrytown. One of those bolts struck the cupola of Goodhue Memorial Hall at Hackley School, igniting a 21-alarm blaze that destroyed nearly 10,000 square feet of the 1903 edifice. Nine classrooms, the archives, and the Kaskel Library were destroyed.

Until that time, Hackley had not contemplated planning for a new library. But the damage was so extensive that the school's buildings and grounds committee, assisted by key administrators and our architects, began weekly meetings to execute the cleanup and, concurrently, to consider the design of a new facility. This initial part of the planning, while simple enough on paper, was complicated by the unique problems associated with excavation within the 100-year-old stone walls. Each week, it seemed as though new problems would arise in how to dispose of the debris at the site while securing the building's valuable stone walls.

Maintain Distinguishing Design Features

The original library featured a dramatic and award-winning design. The ceiling was triple height, and the northwest end was ornamented with stained glass windows. Half of the stacks were contained on a perimeter mezzanine that encircled the entire main level, accessed by a double-wing stairway. Other stacks were distributed under the mezzanine on the main floor. The main floor also contained worktables, the back office, and the reference desk.

The design team met frequently with the constituency base, which included the librarians and faculty of the school, with alumni, students, and parents participating as well. It quickly became evident that key features, such as the building's generous windows and its lofty ceiling, were prized elements that, if possible, should be replicated. Worktables were important and necessary, but we needed noise mitigation for quiet study. One of the most important components was to incorporate the nine lost classrooms (including those for technology) into the reconstructed building.

An Opportunity for Expansion

Hackley's leadership determined ultimately that this devastating setback could be an opportunity if funding beyond the insurance reimbursement could be obtained. After months of discussion, planning, and site analysis, it was agreed that the original single-story building could be reconstructed as two stories. In addition, the original ridge of the roof in the central space was sufficiently high to create a double-height space with a vaulted ceiling for the central reading room. Such an approach would allow the school to reestablish some of the best features of the old library, while more than doubling the usable space of the building to 16,860 square feet.

An extensive opportunity/constraint analysis followed. The school's long-term space goals were considered in order to reach consensus about which academic departments might move into potential new spaces on the first floor, below the library. The design team visited several schools to study the layouts of their libraries, particularly the placement of technology spaces. The team noted that many schools and universities place technology and information science spaces either contiguous to or actually inside of their libraries; this provided a likely path for Hackley. We also needed a space for our frequent board of trustees meetings and an informal space for students. It was decided that one wing on the second floor would contain a technology suite within the library space, and that the lower floors of both wings would contain the school's history department. Under the main reading room of the library, a reception area and student lounge would frame the elegant staircase that would lead to the second-floor library.

Materials and Resources

With the space needs settled, the requirements of a functioning library were addressed. Lost in the fire were 35,000 volumes, but with many resources

Goodhue Memorial Hall with connector to Raymond Hall

available digitally, future needs were predicted at less than half of that number. The architects worked closely with the librarians to imagine where stacks could be situated to be serviceable and aesthetically appropriate. It was also envisioned that display areas for archival materials would be important, along with glass-front cabinets for the media collection. The additional 8,800 square feet allowed for all of these features.

The library staff consists of two librarians and one assistant. However, room for additional staff seemed logical. To that end, a staff workroom with three workstations was included. The director has her own office, with the central copier in her anteroom. The reception desk seats two or three staff members; this allows for flexibility and potential staff expansion.

Student workspaces were the highest priority, and the library was designed to accommodate a variety of student arrangements. The main reading room, with the barrel-vaulted ceiling, was divided by the central placement of the reception desk. On the southeast side, comfortable furniture was arranged for students to relax and work. On the northwest side were large tables that served student needs and also could be rearranged for meetings of the board of trustees. Computers for student use were located in the workstations along both corridor wings, which are perpendicular to the main reading room. In addition, six study alcoves (four with glass walls) were incorporated in the east and west wings.

A Learning Process

In order to make the most productive use of the library's individual spaces, trade-offs were inevitable. Hackley was intent on retaining the open-space feel of the original structure, as well as the aesthetics of huge windows with expansive views. These considerations raised noise abatement and heating/cooling issues. Another concern was how a small staff of librarians could complete their everyday work and, at the same time, have the ability to monitor the students to make sure they were on task. While not all of these situations were met completely, the end result showed that attention was paid to the more important factors—primarily, that the students were served, which needed to be the dominant outcome of this plan.

The lessons learned from this unexpected, arduous, yet fulfilling process were many:

- Take the time to plan carefully.
- Confer widely and ask questions twice or even three times.
- Be sure that members of the team look at all the ideas and comment on them.
- Don't be afraid to think big and to venture beyond your comfort zone.
- Most of all, keep your objectives in mind; do not compromise.

Philip Variano is associate head of school at Hackley School in Tarrytown, New York.

The Design

The Iconic Library Building Represents the Spirit of Hackley

By **PETER GISOLFI**

HACKLEY IS A K-THROUGH-12 INDEPENDENT SCHOOL, located on a 280-acre site in Tarrytown, New York. The school was founded as a preparatory school for boys; today it serves a coeducational population of approximately 900 students. The library at Hackley was located in Goodhue Memorial Hall, a neoclassical stone building that previously was the assembly hall for the school. In 1983, the central portion of the one-story building was converted to a library for high school and middle school students. This building has been the iconic heart of the campus for more than 100 years.

A fire, started by lightning, destroyed the wood structure and the wood interior of Goodhue Memorial Hall, leaving only the masonry shell of the building. After a three-year design and con-

struction process, the transformed stone building reopened with a new second level and a somewhat larger footprint that doubled the size of the original building. The new Sternberg Library occupies the entire second floor; classrooms, faculty offices, and a student lounge are located on the first floor; and mechanical spaces and the school archives are on the basement level. Goodhue resumed its position as the iconic building that most identifies Hackley.

Program Requirements

We worked with a small building committee that included the head of the school, the assistant head of the school, the business manager, members of the board of trustees, the construction manager, and the architects and landscape architects. The building committee met weekly and reported periodically to the board of trustees. The committee established the following program requirements:

- Create a new library of approximately 8,000 square feet for high school and middle school students.
- Consider replacing the original one-story building with a two-story building, which would double the interior space to approximately 16,000 square feet.
- Design an incombustible building.
- On the first floor, accommodate classrooms, faculty offices, and a student lounge adjacent to the central stair that leads to the second-floor library.

Design Objectives

The building committee established the following design objectives:

- Restore the exterior appearance of the original stone building.
- Transform the interior space.
- Use neoclassical detail to emulate the interior of the original building.
- Design the library for transparency between the various spaces.
- Design the library for easy management by a professional staff of two or three.
- Create a grand reading room with a barrel-vaulted ceiling at the center of the building.
- Reestablish the heart of the Hackley campus.

Goodhue Memorial Hall as seen from Akin Common after restoration and expansion.
Inset: Goodhue seen from Akin Common after the fire in August 2007.

Cross-section through the new two-story library

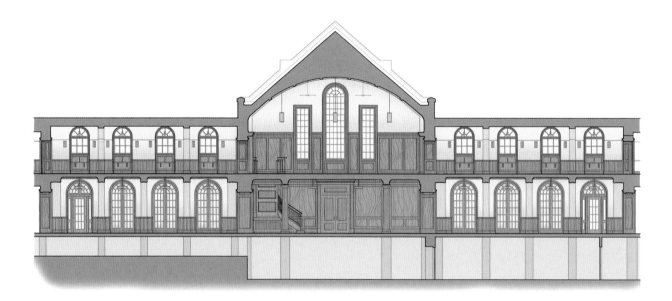

Longitudinal section through the new two-story library

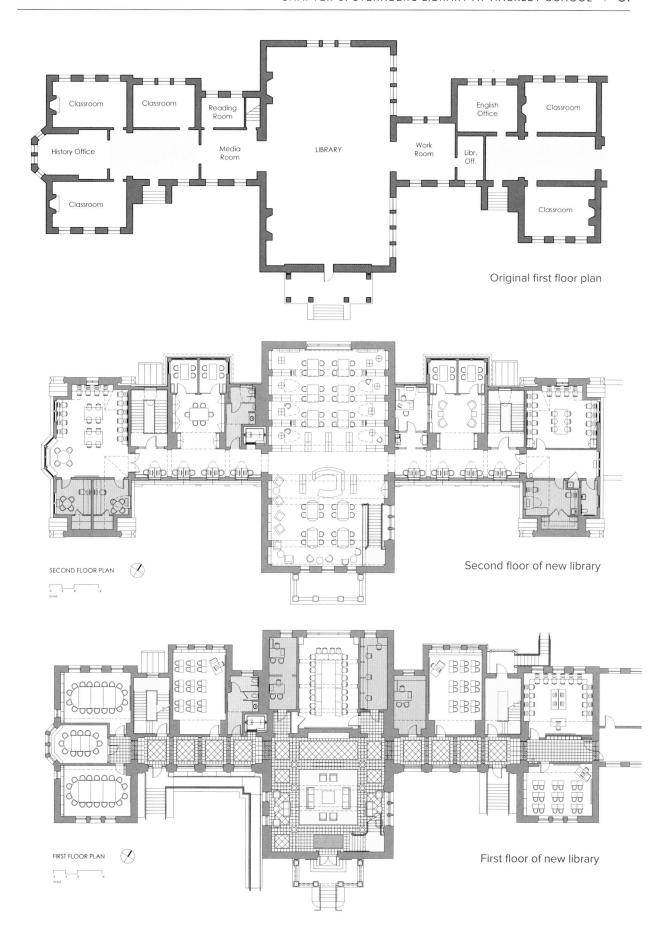

Original first floor plan

SECOND FLOOR PLAN

SCALE

Second floor of new library

FIRST FLOOR PLAN

SCALE

First floor of new library

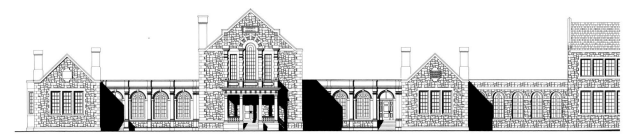

Original southeast elevation

(Left) Original library in Goodhue Memorial Hall after the fire; (right) Sternberg Library under construction with new steel structure

New Plan

The design of the interior space was inspired by two elements: the centrally located barrel-vaulted ceiling of the original assembly hall, and the single-loaded corridors facing the main quadrangle. (Single-loaded corridors serve classrooms, offices, and other interior spaces on one side of the corridor and look to the outdoors on the other side.)

On the first floor, the main entry opens to a spacious student lounge and an open stair leading to the library above. The corridors on either side of the lounge are single-loaded and are transparent to the main quadrangle on the southeast.

The new second-floor space is occupied entirely by the Sternberg Library; the concrete slab of the second floor is tied to the new steel structure and also to the stone walls at the perimeter. Creating a

second floor was made possible by the prodigious height of the original one-story building. The flanking wings of the second floor were created by raising the roof with copper dormers.

The main reading room is distinguished by a steel-framed, barrel-vaulted ceiling of acoustically absorbing plaster; the ceiling resembles the barrel vault of the original assembly space. On either side of the central space are student workstations overlooking the main quadrangle to the southeast; adjacent to the workstations are glass-enclosed group study spaces facing northwest, as well as instructional space and offices for the librarians and the information technology staff—all transparent to each other. The library was designed to foster collaborative learning; it is not a silent space.

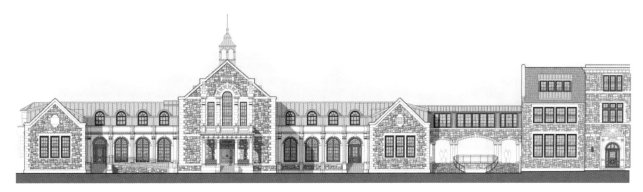

Southeast elevation after transformation

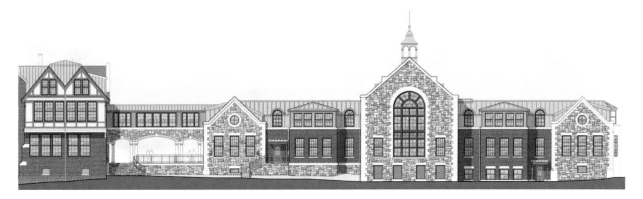

Northwest elevation after transformation

Green Initiatives

The green initiatives for Goodhue are extraordinary.

- Goodhue Memorial is a gold LEED-certified building.
- In order to assure the stability of the stone walls, a new steel structure was inserted on the inside of the stone. This created space for 10 to 15 inches of spray foam insulation, which increases the thermal resistance of the walls from R-4 to R-30, and the roof from R-4 to R-50. This amount of insulation provides a stable interior climate.
- The original windows were single-glazed with significant infiltration. The new wood windows are double-glazed with effective weather stripping.

- New energy-efficient lighting provides further savings.
- Goodhue is heated and cooled with a closed-loop geothermal system, drilled into solid rock. This system has the capacity to heat and cool approximately 50,000 square feet—the area of three buildings on the main quadrangle.
- The new building of 16,000 square feet uses approximately only 20 percent of the energy of the original building, which was only 8,000 square feet. On a square-foot basis, energy consumption has been reduced by about 90 percent.

Collaborative Strategies

When the building committee began working on the reconstruction of Goodhue Memorial Hall, the key players had already collaborated successfully on multiple projects for almost ten years. Their previous projects included a campus master plan, the reconfiguration of the access roads, three new buildings—a middle school, a lower school, and a science building—and significant landscape enhancements. The success of this collaboration was based on the following:

- The appropriate people were present at the table, including the head of the school, the assistant head of the school, the business manager, board members, the construction manager, and the architects.
- We engaged in healthy debate in a trusting environment, where no one felt shy about speaking up.
- The members of the building committee were intellectually and emotionally committed to Hackley. The board members were Hackley alumni; the administrators had been at the school for many years; and the design professionals, having already completed many projects at the school, were familiar with the culture of the institution and the overall campus plan.

Achieving Success

Perhaps the most significant success in connection with the Sternberg Library is locating it at the center of the school, facing the main quadrangle and Akin Common. Goodhue Memorial Hall is now a natural destination, an active space that is filled with students at all times.

Our obligation as stewards of the planet is to transform older buildings into energy-efficient structures. Goodhue Memorial Hall has been converted to a completely up-to-date structure with innovative mechanical systems; at the same time, significant aspects of the building's history have been preserved and restored.

New reading room

Collaborative study alcoves accommodate three student groups

The Impact

The Sternberg Library at Hackley: After a Fire, Renewal

By **BRIANNA JUDKINS**

AFTER THREE YEARS IN TEMPORARY SPACE, THE NEW Sternberg Library opened in fall 2010. Visitors who climb the large staircase that leads from the first floor of the building up to the library enter a stunning open space of relaxed grandeur.

The library is the highlight of any school tour. Entering the main reading room, visitors are impressed. One student stated, "I love that it has an open design, yet has traditional elements that make it clear this is a library." The large window at the northwest side of the library overlooks much of the campus—Akin Common, the lower school, and the middle school. You can also see students walking to and from the gymnasium and the auditorium, or just playing outside.

The furniture offers a mix of traditional and relaxed options. The comfortable easy chairs and padded stools are an enticement for students who want to work alone or read for pleasure; students working in small groups choose traditional tables and chairs. The circulation/reference desk also conveys a mix of traditional and relaxed options. Its purpose is clear, but the comfortable stools placed at the back of the desk make it a great place for librarians to work with individuals or small groups of students.

Books are prominent in the design of the library, but because many information resources are now accessed digitally, shelf space has been reduced significantly. Librarians are thoughtful in what they order and are diligent about weeding the collection.

Large Windows for Brightness and Views

The new library is bright and airy. Large windows welcome sunlight throughout the day, and they also offer great views. One student said, "Looking out the large windows in the main area is a great way to let your mind wander when you need a break." Another mused, "If I want to see if it is going to rain, I come to the library because it has the best view of approaching clouds." Even the lighting fixtures in the library elicited comments. One group of students claimed that the library "has the best lighting in the school." Bookcase and accent lighting showcase the library's custom woodwork and simple yet stately detail. The white oak motif is consistent throughout, lending a warmth that combines tradition and modernity.

The library is easily accessible from multiple entry points. When it first opened, three different staircases led to the library. Since then, an enclosed bridge has been constructed to connect the second floor of the main upper school building directly to the library. The four entry points have made the library the social hub of the upper school. One student observed, "The large atrium-like open space of the main room creates a feeling of community, and everyone is just drawn to it." The library was clearly designed for access and open movement.

The four study rooms in the two wings can accommodate small groups of students and are always in use. Students can work collaboratively on projects or study for exams together. At various times of the day, when the library is crowded, these rooms serve as quiet spaces where students can work without being disturbed.

Class in Sternberg Library

The alcoves adjacent to the study rooms on the east and west sides of the main reading room include shelving for specialized collections, some that are unique to our school. One alcove houses plays, short stories, graphic novels, and books written by Hackley alumni; the other contains our collections devoted to professional development, parenting, health and wellness, and textbooks. Additionally, we have created a periodicals reading area in the west alcove for print newspapers and magazines. DVDs are housed behind two large glass doors in the main reading room.

DESIGN TEAM
Peter Gisolfi
Klaus Kalmbach
Kenneth Pojman
Sandra Mintzes
Ronen Wilk
Joori Suh
Crosby Scott

PHOTOGRAPHY BY
Robert Mintzes

Advanced Technology

Each of the two wings of the library features eight computer workstations for patron use. As students have begun using personal devices in the library, the use of desktop computers has dropped; nevertheless, they are important for students who need to use specific software programs or to print a document. For students who bring their own devices, floor outlets throughout the library are easily accessible for charging them. The library's copy machine and printer for upper school students are always in use, and supplies such as tape, scissors, and staplers are nearby.

Computer labs at the far ends of the library provide areas for classes to meet for instruction in technology, using a Smart Board. With computer labs located inside the library, students can use electronic databases and print resources simultaneously.

The school's history department is located on the first floor of the building; this allows for easy collaboration between history teachers and librarians. Using the elevator, carts filled with books can be delivered from the library directly to history classrooms.

The library workroom was designed for behind-the-scenes efficiency. An oversized closet houses all of the supplies needed to cover, repair, and process books. The library workroom also provides two desks for library staff, a sink, and storage for professional journals and books.

A Redefined Library

The library fire was a huge loss for the Hackley community, but what has been created in its place has redefined the library at the school. The nooks and crannies of the old library, while cherished by some alumni, have been amply upgraded to generate new memories and new learning experiences for our students. This new and inviting space of relaxed grandeur should serve the needs of the Hackley community well into the future.

Brianna Judkins was appointed head librarian at Hackley in 2011.

Digital carrels in Sternberg Library

New computer lab

Library overlooks the large quadrangle, Akin Common

The Planning Process

The Vision for the New Library Takes a Classical Form

By **MICHAEL V. MCGILL**

TO UNDERSTAND THE THINKING BEHIND THE DESIGN OF THE NEW SCARSDALE High School library, we have to go back in time. Historically, most high school libraries were relatively small spaces that housed a limited collection of books and accommodated a relatively small number of students who either read silently or did research under the watchful eye of an adult librarian. Practically speaking, libraries were peripheral to the education of large numbers of pupils.

In the late 1960s and the 1970s, this old model began to evolve into a hybrid of traditional and newer forms; forward-looking teachers placed greater emphasis on research, especially in the social sciences, and students began to do more group and cooperative work. By the 1990s, the typical high school library continued to be a place for reading and research, but it also accommodated more student collaboration as well as increased enrollment, albeit in a limited space. As a result, if you'd headed to the library in any number of America's secondary schools in 1995 or 1996, you would have found some students talking about their class work, some socializing in conversational tones, and others try-ing to study. You might have wondered how anyone could get anything done amidst the clatter. Adults would be trying their best to offer educational support and monitor noise levels, while possibly attempting to maintain separate "talking" and "quiet" zones.

Technological Changes Imapct Library Design

Meanwhile, technological changes were raising questions about the library's role and function. Computers were becoming more integrated into regular academic instruction. The stationary computer station was giving way to the laptop. Some experts foresaw a

93

future when there would be no need for a centralized library, because every student would have a personal device; research and collaboration would simply require a decentralized constellation of wired workspaces in each building. Such was the context for discussions of a renovated Scarsdale High School library.

In fact, the topic had been the subject of speculation for years. A major building program in the 1930s had placed the library more or less at the center of the school. But in the 1970s, when the school building stretched for nearly a quarter of a mile down the Post Road, the library migrated to a new science wing at the far north end. Almost immediately, some found the new space inadequate. Retrospectively, for example, the former Scarsdale superintendent Harold Howe (subsequently U.S. commissioner of education) observed with asperity that he'd wanted to build a larger space under an abutting parking lot and field. "But the idea never went anywhere," he mused. "I guess people in Scarsdale like their trees."

By the late 1990s, rising enrollment had prompted the board of education to consider a bond issue—the first in years—that would ultimately fund a new library. Scarsdale's elementary schools were under immediate pressure, and the high school had been growing incrementally. The first big wave of students would arrive in the near future.

Why new construction? Enrollments in the 1970s had already been as high as those projected for the 2000s, so the building should have been large enough to accommodate the added number of students. But special education, computer instruction, and other new programs had taken up space that became available when enrollments dropped in the 1980s. Women's sports made new demands on limited athletic space; science labs were tightly packed, and some science courses had fewer than the full complement of labs.

The 1970s library—the one that fell short of Harold Howe's standards—was an L-shaped open space on the third floor of a semi-Brutalist addition to the 1930s Gothic Revival building at the core of the campus. It was a structure replete with tracery, pointed arches, faux buttresses, and a central tower. As I recall the room I first saw sometime in 1998, it had a low ceiling, few windows, fluorescent lighting that attempted to stave off the dim interior, and rumpled moss-green wall-to-wall carpeting. High stacks stood in the short leg of the "L," while the long leg held shorter stacks and tables. The library was filled to overflowing with students and was often noisy.

A "Domino" Construction Strategy

Considering the challenges at the high school, the architects and a committee of professional staff and parents devised a "domino" construction strategy that involved both new construction and the renovation of existing spaces. A new, large gymnasium at the south end of the building would free up an existing gym close to the center. That gym (from the 1930s) would become the new library. In turn, the 1970s library in the science wing would become classroom and laboratory space.

This strategy led to more specific discussions of each of the new spaces, with the library posing especially interesting issues. The planning team would have to wrestle with relatively familiar questions about how the library would support instruction, as well as the type and location of seating and stacks. Team participants also found themselves confronting rapid technological changes that had unclear parameters, and whose ultimate implications could not be known. How would students learn in 2020? What role would the library play in their education? What would the library of the future look like?

The answers to these questions were necessarily provisional. The planning team's underlying impulse was to preserve the best of existing practice while providing flexibility for innovation in the future. Inevitably, some of the resulting decisions were wiser than others.

Firmly grounded in classical forms, the architects argued for transforming the high-ceilinged gymnasium into a large, two-story space with a central atrium. The first level would provide ample reading space, plus workspace featuring fixed computers. The large middle area would include some lower stacks, while high stacks would be off to the sides. The second level would contain more stacks and reading space. To this point, the library appeared traditional, but the planning committee also attached classroom and dedicated computer space to the upstairs level that ringed the atrium. The assumption was that students would work on the Internet or word-process at the fixed stations downstairs, while teachers would continue to bring whole classes to the library and work with them upstairs.

With the somewhat claustrophobic atmosphere of the 1970s library in mind, the planners sought to make the new space light and airy by capitalizing on the old gym's long Gothic windows, installing uplit chandeliers in place of fluorescent tubes, and creating clerestory windows near the ceiling.

The emphasis on light and space was also a response to the mixed activities in the 1970s library—students who were collaborating, socializing, reading, or doing research could be mutually incompatible and sometimes noisy. The theory was that a less crowded, more gracious space would invite civilized behavior. Students who wanted to read or work more quietly would have added room on the second floor. And adult work areas at opposite ends of the room on each level would provide passive supervision of the students.

Library Combines Dedicated Space and Open Space

Almost twenty years on, the decision to make the library central to the school once again, and to adhere to classical form—in a combination of dedicated and open space that allowed for different activities—appears to have been sound. Today, teachers are advising students to use both the printed and digitized materials as well as the human resources that are available in the library. If anything, expert professional advice, communal spaces, and areas tailored for collaboration are even more important at a time when technology can so easily isolate users from direct human interaction.

What the committee did not fully anticipate was the degree to which the laptop would transform work and associated space requirements. If the fixed desktop computer hasn't entirely given way to the personal device, it seems poised to do so; much of what students do on the computer can occur in different settings throughout the day. Nor did the committee fully appreciate the degree to which the library would attract even more students in the 2000s than it did before. Although Scarsdale's new library was significantly larger than its 1970s predecessor, demand soon outran capacity during periods of peak use.

These realities do not devalue what Scarsdale educators, parents, and architects accomplished at the turn of the current century. Rather, they compelled us to expand our vision of the school library, to imagine how a more classical form can connect with the flow into other spaces where, supported by technology, students and teachers can investigate, collaborate, and innovate. In short, we can now see that the planning process we started in the late 1990s was only a beginning.

Michael V. McGill was superintendent of the Scarsdale schools from 1998 to 2014.

New library at Scarsdale High School

The Design

A Gymnasium Becomes
an Academic Library

By **PETER GISOLFI**

SCARSDALE HIGH SCHOOL IS LOCATED ON A CAMPUS of approximately fifty acres in the center of the village of Scarsdale in Westchester County, New York. The school is located between two north-south roads: Route 22 (a state road) on the eastern boundary, and Brewster Road (a village road) on the western boundary. The high school building was constructed in the 1910s with add-ons in the 1930s, 1960s, 1990s, and 2000s.

In 2004 we began designing a new library, to be located in an early twentieth-century dou-ble-height gymnasium, which is positioned above the cafeteria at the western-facing center of the school. Our work in 2004 also included construct-ing a new gymnasium, football field, and track at the southern end of the campus. This expansion made it unnecessary to maintain the older gymna-sium, which was an ideal place for the new library because of its prominent central location.

Scarsdale is a renowned public high school that serves approximately 1,600 students. The environ-ment is competitive, both academically and socially.

Program Requirements

The program requirements for the new library were straightforward:

- Build a centrally located library in the former gymnasium space situated on the second floor, above the cafeteria.
- Construct a two-story library of about 12,800 square feet that includes seating, books, flexible instructional spaces, and offices for librarians and staff.
- Accommodate a book collection of approximately 40,000 volumes.
- Consider expanding the footprint of the existing gymnasium and cafeteria.
- Assume that the main entrance of the library will be on the gymnasium floor level, but include an exit from the mezzanine level to the adjacent, third-floor corridors.

Design Objectives

The library design committee, made up of administrators, librarians, and architects, established the following objectives:

- Locate the library at the center of school, physically and academically.
- Make the library a natural destination.
- Make the library transparent and easy to supervise.
- Design the library to be compatible with the architecture of the early twentieth-century building.

New Plan

The plan for the library is derived from the simple 60 × 90-foot rectangle of the original gymnasium. The library became an elongated space, running east-west, with additional space facing north. That space is actually a three-level addition with 1,000

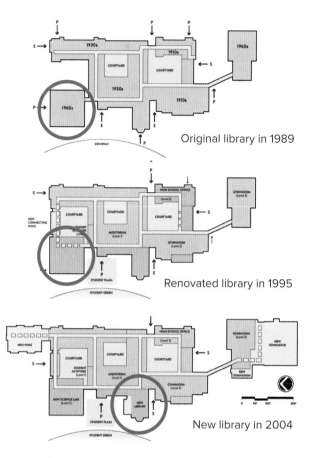

Original library in 1989

Renovated library in 1995

New library in 2004

square feet at each level—the cafeteria level, the main floor of the library, and the mezzanine level. The added space on both levels of the library is used predominately for instruction.

The mezzanine level surrounds the main floor of the library; there is an open rectangular space, which is double height when viewed from the main level. With this configuration, most of the library can be seen from both the main and mezzanine levels. Above the 20 × 60-foot opening in the mezzanine floor is a new raised roof, which allows for clerestory light from all four directions—north, south, east, and west. The mezzanine is connected to the main level by two open staircases.

To ensure passive observation of virtually the entire library, there are two glass-enclosed librarian offices at the western end of the mezzanine and main levels. The circulation desk is at the eastern end of the main level, adjacent to the library entrance.

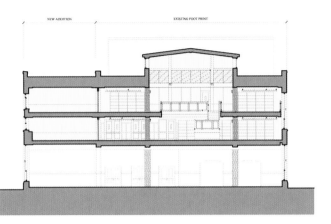

Original gymnasium above the cafeteria

Transformed library above the cafeteria

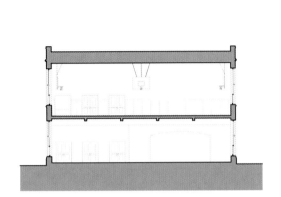

Transformed high school library. Inset: Gymnasium before it became the library.

Green Initiatives

- Unsatisfactory aluminum-frame windows from the 1980s were replaced by higher-quality, double-glazed windows.
- The windows in the clerestory and in the three-story addition are also double-glazed.
- Generous windows facing north and south, as well as the clerestory light from above, provide the library with daylight throughout the school day.
- The new construction, including the roof, clerestory, and the new classrooms to the north, is well insulated.

Collaborative Strategies

The design work for this project was overseen by two committees. The first of these was a library design committee, which included the superintendent of schools, the high school principal, two senior librarians, the head of facilities, the assistant superintendent for business, and the architects. This committee met approximately every two weeks, or as needed, to review the details of the library portion of the bond project.

The second committee was the school bond committee, which included the superintendent of schools, the assistant superintendent for business, the head of facilities, and representatives of the board of education, as well as local volunteers with expertise in construction. This committee met every Friday at 8 a.m. to manage the entire $60-million school bond project.

In collaborating with the library design committee, we typically examined alternatives to determine the best choices. For example, I was able to demonstrate that the librarians and staff would have a better view of the whole space in a two-level library with a mezzanine than they would in a single-level library.

Achieving Success

In a complicated setting, with many voices to be heard, there were significant positive results:

- The new library serves the students at a variety of scales: students working independently, students collaborating on projects (which often require research), and students taking advantage of instruction opportunities in the two new library classrooms.
- The library is located at the geographic center of the school, reinforced by the proximity of the cafeteria. The auditorium, the auditorium lobby, the cafeteria, and the library form the center of the western side of the school.
- Transparency within the library is achieved with the elongated opening to the mezzanine, and in a series of details: glass railings, glass partitions on the librarians' offices, and glass partitions on the interior walls of the instructional spaces. The interior space of the library is either continuously open or transparent because of the use of glass. (The library setting could be improved if similar transparency connected the public corridor to the main level of the library.)
- The transformation of the original gymnasium is successful. A new space has been formed, but aspects of the original gymnasium design remain, including window locations, interior brick walls, and other details.
- The library has become a prominent feature of the building exterior, visible to all at the center of the Brewster Road façade.
- The 12,800-square-foot library is constantly occupied by students. It is an active place—a community center for Scarsdale High School.

Lower and upper levels of the main reading room

The Impact

New Teaching and Learning Spaces Attract Students, Teachers, and the Community

By **PHYLLIS DIBIANCO**

WHEN I JOINED THE STAFF OF THE SCARSDALE HIGH School library, I found myself immersed in a tradition of intensive library-based research in English, social studies, world languages, the sciences, and even mathematics. Students were required to devise their own inquiry-based research projects, even before this became the mantra of school librarians.

Teachers eagerly introduced themselves, showed me samples of assignments and student work, and competed for times to bring their classes into our one instructional space that was, in fact, located far from resources. Four computers for patron use were in the reference area, none in the classroom. Among other drawbacks, poor sight lines impeded proper supervision, and the antiquated electri-

cal service and network wiring were inadequate to power enough computers to meet the demand. Adding to the congestion, the library, it seemed, was "the place" for students to go during their free time. Many would hide in the study carrels with their lunches to get homework done before they headed to sports practice or after-school clubs. Others met friends in the library to "work" together and socialize.

Clearly, a multipurpose, flexible library was needed for everyday activities, including class research, small group study, collaboration between teachers and librarians, the escalating technological needs of our patrons, browsing the collections, and just socializing.

Meeting the Challenge

The immediate challenge facing the library design committee was to convert a traditional 1930s gymnasium into a two-level public high school library—a main floor with a mezzanine for additional space. To that end, we explored the following issues:

- How to allocate space for staff, equipment, and various print and media collections that support curriculum and student needs.
- How to provide access to our large, well-used book collection (more than 40,000 volumes) on two levels, and also offer flexible spaces for study, class research, and common areas.
- How to design flexible spaces that would accommodate the rapidly changing technology needs of our students.
- In a related matter, how to encourage students to make use of the reliable online databases available in the library and discourage the use of untrustworthy websites that were emerging.

Meetings with faculty, students, community members, and library staff provided various perspectives for the new space at a time when information technology was surging. Site visits to recently renovated high school libraries clarified what would and would not work at Scarsdale High School.

Impact of the New Spaces

All of the spaces in the new library are seemingly in constant use. But perhaps the most identifiable impact of the transformed library is provided by the two newly created teaching and learning spaces. Within two years of completion, the number of classes held in the two bright and spacious library classrooms tripled. Simultaneous with the classroom activity, librarians can assist students using reference materials and online resources, and teachers can work with groups or individual students, with none of the activities hindering any of the others.

The two classrooms are equipped with twenty-five digital workstations for students, a teaching station with an interactive whiteboard, and tables and chairs on casters to accommodate flexible arrangements for student collaboration, discussion groups, and small group activities. We found that as students shifted the furniture, they personalized the space and became more engaged in their activities.

The glass walls between the classrooms and the library center provide the transparency that librarians need to see into the classrooms and respond if help is needed. With scanners, printers, and projectors in each classroom, students can make copies of primary resources for individual research and presentations. Instruction on academic database use prepares students and teachers for at-home access.

The seminar room on the mezzanine level is furnished with a projection station and laptops. Small groups of eight to ten students can use this space. The room's location on the upper level behind the book stacks avoids distractions from the usual comings and goings that take place in a busy library. Small study groups, testing, teacher and staff collaboration, and community group meetings take place there during and after school. The room is wired with assistive technology and has elevator access; these accommodations expand our services to the entire community. The seminar room is a cozy, quiet, out-of-the-way place we had not anticipated.

Staff Spaces

The main floor includes a large circulation desk staffed by aides who assist students and teachers. A workroom is used for processing and repairing materials. A secretary's office, which is glass-enclosed, provides views of our teenagers—their work habits as well as their antics.

Near the circulation desk is a staff bathroom. The adjacent kitchenette serves the needs of the staff as well as community activities that occur during and after school.

Librarian offices are glass-enclosed, providing visibility for easy supervision of activity throughout the library and, most importantly, these offices offer a welcoming presence. Our doors are open, we are visible, and students and staff are comfortable coming to us for help in locating resources or just asking us to recommend a good book.

Unanticipated Issues

A two-story library offered opportunities for expanded and flexible spaces, and some constraints.

When the reconstruction was complete, daylight from the clerestory windows brightened the center area of the library, but we discovered acoustical issues created by the mezzanine. Voices were amplified, carrying up from the center area to the mezzanine level. To remedy the situation, we moved the student worktables to the reference area under the mezzanine, and we moved the computers to the center area for student use during free time.

Originally, the mezzanine was furnished with large worktables for student use, but that area invited loud conversation that disturbed others. We replaced the tables in the mezzanine with study carrels. Tables work well in the periodicals area.

Occasionally, teenage students see the balcony as an opportunity to toss things to friends below.

An entrance/exit on the mezzanine level was impractical because the circulation desk and security system are on the main level. We designated the exit door on the mezzanine level as an emergency exit.

A Positive Outcome

The new library at Scarsdale High School is an active space that serves the needs of students, teachers, administrators, and community residents.

- Library instruction has been transformed by the two large classrooms that provide spaces for teaching, exhibits, departmental meetings, teacher instruction through the Scarsdale Teachers Institute, and parent training sessions, all of which further community involvement in the high school.
- Parents are comfortable in these surroundings. They learn about the library's resources in order to help their children access the online catalog and databases from home. Many join our parent volunteer group.
- Furniture on the main floor's center area is easily moved to create an inviting atmosphere for poetry readings, guest speakers, and other performances.
- The landings on the staircases have featured music and poetry performances, enabling us to take advantage of the unique acoustics. Voices project throughout the library without amplification.
- With improved sight lines, the library is easily supervised on both levels.

When Scarsdale High School alumni return for a reunion, the tour always includes the library, which is now the centerpiece of the school. They ooh and aah as they enter the light-filled central area. They marvel at the activity generated by students and teachers, and they acknowledge the welcoming feeling created here.

DESIGN TEAM
Peter Gisolfi
Kenneth Pojman
Jackie Ashton
Jenny Le

PHOTOGRAPHY BY
Norman McGrath
Robert Mintzes

Phyllis DiBianco was librarian at Scarsdale High School from 1997 to 2013, and head district librarian from 2009 to 2013.

The Expansion and Transformation of a Residential College Library

By **JOHN LOGE**

ARLY IN THE 1990S, YALE UNIVERSITY DECIDED TO RENOVATE ITS TWELVE RESidential colleges. Most of the residential colleges were built during the 1920s and 1930s, and maintenance had been deferred for years. The mechanical systems were original, and all living and social spaces, including our college library, were showing their age. There was no ADA accessibility.

The colleges were reconstructed, one by one. When Timothy Dwight College's turn finally came many years later, it was under construction for two summers and the intervening year. During that academic year, Timothy Dwight students and staff were moved to a temporary dormitory that had been built a few years before, specifically to house students during the renovation of their college.

Timothy Dwight, like the other residential colleges, has its own library in a privileged space. Ours was just off the foyer of the main entrance, on the second floor near the common room and the dining hall—the two primary gathering places in the college. Access was by an open staircase from the foyer. When the uses of the various rooms and

areas within the college changed over the years to accommodate other activities and the changing interests and needs of students, our college library stayed on the second floor.

The main room was still showing some of its former appeal with its several long tables, built-in shelving, oiled pine paneling, and windows that overlooked the college courtyard. At the rear of this main room were two small rooms that looked and felt as though they had been added sometime after 1935, one behind the other with old steel shelving and 1950s-style maple furniture and study carrels. With an increase in the student population since 1935 and even with the extension of these two rooms, our library was too small to accommodate students who used

105

it for quiet study, especially during midterms and finals. With the advent of laptop computers, the table space and electrical outlets were increasingly inadequate. And, of course, after the many years of use by active college students, the library was quite worn and unappealing.

Our Turn for Renovation

When it was our turn for reconstruction, the entire Timothy Dwight community—students, faculty fellows, and staff at all levels—heartily welcomed the opportunity to restore the college's beauty and renovate its functions to benefit all of us. As one would expect, the university formed a high-level physical plant committee to interview and select an architect. I was invited to the meetings and presentations for the Timothy Dwight selection, and to our delight, Peter Gisolfi Associates was selected. He shared our feeling that the restoration should follow as much as possible the aesthetics that James Gamble Rogers had in mind when he designed the college in the Federal style in 1935:

red brick, milled wood paneling, pegged wooden floors, double-hung windows, period fixtures, and appropriate architectural details. The architects promised that their work would be seamless with the original James Gamble Rogers design.

When the design process began, the architects consulted Timothy Dwight students and staff about their needs and preferences for particular rooms and areas—offices, student rooms, dining facilities, recreational spaces, and, of course, our college library. They met with us privately, in small groups, and with our student college council made up of eight students, two elected from each class, whose meetings are routinely open to all students in the college. We felt listened to and heard, and we freely voiced our opinions about the library's inadequate size, the functional arrangement of rooms, and accessibility to the college's public areas. The architects suggested that the two study rooms at the rear could be converted to a student room with the entrance located away from the library.

The first floor, which included a room for watching TV and a men's room, became the first floor of

"Town Hall" entry to the Timothy Dwight College library

The middle level of the library was originally the coat room and restrooms.

the library. It looked just like the second floor, with inset shelving and wooden panels and floors, areas of comfortable upholstered chairs, and large, rectangular tables for studying and laptops. After the library was completed, one would never guess that the new first-floor addition to the library was not part of the original 1935 design. A former unused crawl space below the first floor was excavated to create a spacious area to house desktop computers and printers for students who did not own a personal computer and printer.

Connecting the Levels: A Striking Staircase

To connect these three levels was, perhaps, the most appealing and striking feature of our restored and expanded library: a staircase. It traveled up the wall that faced the courtyard with its generous windows. The architectural banister and semicircular shape of the staircase effectively made the three levels into one large room. (An elevator was installed to make the library accessible at all three levels.) Once the books were returned to their shelves, we had a library with an abundance of daylight and a variety of welcoming spots to settle in and study.

When students and staff moved back into our college, we were happy to be home. Our college had been transformed, and although we were pleased with the new plumbing and weather-tight windows, we were even more delighted to recognize our old college with its look, its feel, and its beauty.

Our expanded library's new staircase is especially appealing. When I would take visitors and graduates on tours of our restored college, I always began with the library, starting at the second floor and walking down, pausing at each level along the way. As we proceeded quietly, with natural light shining through the double-hung widows, students might look up from their studies at one of the rich dark wood tables or a cozy chair, and I would marvel again at the intimate relationship between learning and beauty.

John Loge was dean of Timothy Dwight College at Yale University from 1991 to 2014.

The Design

Student-Run Library Expands to Three Levels

By **PETER GISOLFI**

THE RESIDENTIAL COLLEGES AT YALE UNIVERSITY are modeled after the residential colleges at Oxford and Cambridge universities in England, and each accommodates from 300 to 400 undergraduate students. The important communal spaces at Timothy Dwight College include the dining hall, the common room, and the library, which is open twenty-four hours a day, seven days a week, and is run by students.

In the 1930s design of Timothy Dwight College, the original architect, James Gamble Rogers, located the 940-square-foot library on the second floor, one story above the common room, which is adjacent to the dining hall. Directly below the second-floor library was a coatroom and public restrooms for those using the dining hall. Below the coatroom was an unexcavated crawl space, which accommodated the pipes for the restrooms above.

Program Requirements

The task of my office was to transform, reconstruct, and expand Timothy Dwight College and Rosenfeld Hall, a neighboring early twentieth-century building. The library was a significant factor in the life of the college. But it had been too small originally and was obviously too small for the expanded college that was planned. In addition, with its location on the second floor, the library did not make a clear and direct connection to the other public spaces nearby. We were asked to expand the library as much as possible, and to create flexible space that could accommodate varied furniture arrangements and study areas.

Design Objectives

The design objectives for the project were established in conversations with the head of Timothy Dwight College, the dean of the college, and with Yale's facilities department:

- Seamlessly connect the additional space to the existing library.
- Maintain the style and detail of the original library.
- Make the library visible and accessible from the main entrance on the first floor.
- Visually connect the common room, dining hall, and the library.

- Take advantage of the view from the library to the Timothy Dwight College quadrangle.

New Plan

A simple opportunity for expansion became evident at the beginning of the design process. Because the first-floor coatroom and restrooms occupied the same footprint as the second-floor library, it would be easy to connect those spaces and double the size of the library from 940 to 1,880 square feet. Another option was to transform the existing crawl space that was directly below the original coatroom and restrooms. Although this space was not fully excavated down to basement level, structural investigations revealed that this expansion would be possible. Given the opportunity to reconstruct the crawl space, the university administration, the facilities

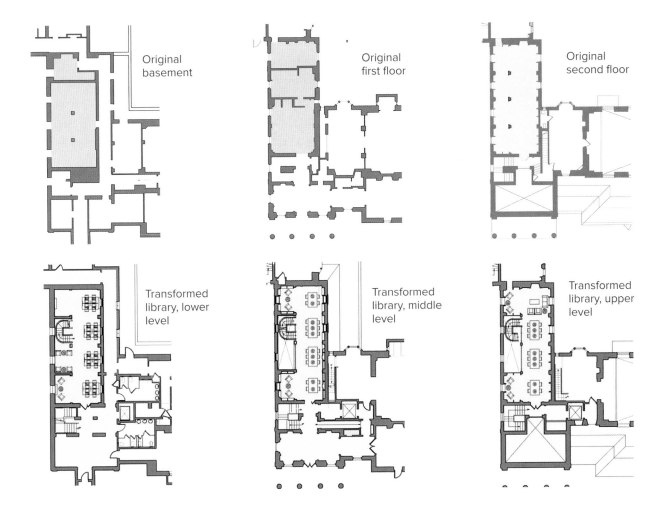

Original basement

Original first floor

Original second floor

Transformed library, lower level

Transformed library, middle level

Transformed library, upper level

department, and representatives from Timothy Dwight College all agreed that a 2,820-square-foot library (expanded two levels below the original library) would be an important asset.

The plan for the new library is straightforward. It occupies three interconnected, light-filled levels, which are served by a winding stair adjacent to the existing windows that overlook the college quadrangle. The top floor incorporates the original Timothy Dwight Library with its barrel-vaulted ceiling; the middle level (formerly the coatroom and restroom space) replicates the woodwork details of the original and provides space for tables and additional shelving for the book collection; the bottom level (formerly unexcavated crawl space) is now at the same elevation as the basement, where many student activity spaces are located. This lowest level of the library, again, was constructed with the finishes and detailing of the original library and provides flexible space that accommodates tables for books and reading, tables for laptops, and comfortable seating for more relaxed work.

Green Initiatives

The twelve residential colleges at Yale University were built between 1920 and 1962. The intention of the university was to transform and reconstruct them so they would last for another 100 years, and would incorporate the sustainable strategies that are present in modern-day buildings. These strategies included the following:

- The mechanical systems in Timothy Dwight College were replaced and reconnected to the central heating and cooling plant.
- In winter, steam is produced to heat the college, while in summer, the central plant produces chilled water for cooling.
- The original single-glazed windows were removed, and new double-glazed wood windows were installed throughout the college.

Collaborative Strategies

To assure that the results would meet the needs of the various constituencies, the university established an intensely collaborative design process, which included the following:

- Regular meetings and interaction with the Yale University facilities department
- Regular meetings with the head of the college and the dean of the college
- Smaller group meetings with the various constituencies
- Occasional meetings with the faculty, staff, and student college council
- Occasional reviews with the university president, vice president for facilities, and dean of the school of architecture

Achieving Success

Although two-thirds of the library is new, it appears that the entire library is a Georgian revival space from the 1930s. With this design language, the space is still appropriate for the twenty-first century, and it offers the flexibility to adapt to changing requirements and preferences. The library is used intensively at all times.

With its vertical arrangement, the library connects the college's basement, first floor, and second floor. Adjacent to the library is a three-story staircase that allows students to enter and exit at any of the three levels. The plan establishes a vertical link to the major circulation pathways, and creates a stronger connection between the multilevel library and its counterparts—the common room and the dining hall. The new library has become a significant communal space in Timothy Dwight College.

Second floor after transformation. Inset: Original one-story library

Timothy Dwight Library (before):

A one-story library with the library on the top floor, a coatroom on the middle floor, and unexcavated space in the basement (K. Tanner)

Timothy Dwight Library (after):

Three-story library with connecting stair (K. Tanner)

The Impact

Forging a Sense of Connection between Students, Their Colleagues, and Their Studies

By **ALEX WERRELL**

YALE UNIVERSITY OVERFLOWS WITH LIBRARIES—AND with shelves, books, lamps, armchairs, and power outlets. Students quickly determine their criteria for favorite study spaces and select a haunt. Of the myriad choices, however, the library in Timothy Dwight College is a student favorite. Patient witness to thousands of term papers, flashcards, periodic tables, and dog-eared Victorian novels, the library is the focal point of life in Timothy Dwight. It is central to and emblematic of the spirit of community; it is the heart of the college.

The feeling of community in Timothy Dwight is extraordinary. This is evident from the dining table to the courtyards, from the college's battle cry—"Áshe," a Yoruba word of power for "We make

it happen"—to the motto inscribed above the seal of the Linonian Society in the library: "Amicitia Concordia Soli Noscimus." The words "We alone learn in friendship and harmony" are echoed by the heraldic emblems within the heart of the seal: piety (the pelican feeding her young), learning (the bookcase), peace (the dove perched on an olive branch), courage and loyalty (the dog), and rebirth through knowledge (the phoenix rising from its own ashes). There is perhaps no better catalog of words and images to describe the atmosphere of camaraderie and learning found in Timothy Dwight College.

Most of all, this keystone of college culture is reflected in the library. The library's design captures the spirit of communal learning over sheltered or cloistered study. Rather than working in isolated carrels or sitting tucked away in study rooms, students enter the library to find family-style tables with their peers huddled over textbooks and computers or reading for pleasure. Sounds drift up and down the spiral staircase that connects the three floors of the library. Some students, finished at last with a midterm or final paper, shuffle down to the computer and printer area on the lowest level. The murmur of students gathered in the courtyard trickles in through the windows—cracked open to let in the evening breeze—as, at the same table, one student annotates Milton while flanked by a budding geneticist researching RNA and an art historian, who is almost lost to sight amid flashcards and oversize art books taken from the shelves.

The Timothy Dwight Library embraces the togetherness explicit in its motto: " . . . noscimus" (we learn), not "nosco" (I learn). Students sit at the long tables, bound together in arduous academic labor; others prefer to curl up in comfortable chairs in front of the fireplace, reading a book. We know that—as Aeneas told his sailors—even these long nights in the library will be remembered pleasantly someday.

The design and content of the library yoke the past and present. The redesign has tripled the size of the library, thus opening space for additional volumes and displays of notable works, historical volumes, or interesting discoveries. The inclusion of a display case in the foyer of the library allows the college's student librarians to highlight and emphasize that sense of community. For instance, the various ex libris labels, changed time after time, given to commemorate a graduation or to memorialize a classmate, make up only some of the layers in Yale's storied history. Displayed here, too, are books that were made in the basement on the Timothy Dwight press, which now lives on only in the books it once printed.

One of the notable and, indeed, emotional additions to the library is space for "senior books." Every year, each member of the graduating class recommends a book for the library—adding to the collected volumes, and also to that sense of "friendship and harmony" so essential to the college. Some recommend books that had influenced their studies; others suggest those that had contributed to their personal growth. As such, both Dr. Ruth and Dr. Seuss can be found on the seniors' shelf. The alcove doubles as a workspace and respite. Here, students can look out through the window onto the courtyard and the gingko tree or peruse the shelves to find the inspiration that had stirred the students before them.

The lowest level of the library has become a creative and digital space. At the computers, two architecture students might quibble over the design of a homeless shelter with an eco-roof, while the student across from them—at a long worktable—could be sketching a still-life with a pencil. Students talk quietly and help one another, while learning coaches meet to discuss problem sets and rough drafts with their peers at the opposite end of the room. A larger group of students might pin a map to the wall to discuss a global policy presentation. The space encourages and enables collaboration and discovery.

Computer area on lower level of the library

It can be easy to forget how essential a space is to learning—that is, until you walk into a space that inspires it. The architects crafted a library that deepens a sense of togetherness, not just between students, but also between students and subjects. It was here—by the fireplace on the second floor—that I read Brontë, Chaucer, Milton, and Morrison. It was here at the communal tables that two of my friends fell in love—with chemistry and with one another. Hawthorne wrote that there is "an irresistible and inevitable" connection that compels us to "linger around . . . the spot where some great and marked event has given the color to [our] lifetime." When graduates of Timothy Dwight College return for a reunion or visit, the first destination is the library. They run their fingers over the volumes and across the tables—searching once again for that feeling of friendship and harmony so beautifully expressed in the building itself.

DESIGN TEAM
Peter Gisolfi
Michael Tribe
Klaus Kalmbach
Patricia Montero
Joseph Keating

PHOTOGRAPHY BY
Robert Mintzes

Alex Werrell teaches English at Hopkins School in New Haven, Connecticut. He was the Timothy Dwight student librarian from 2010 to 2013.

Main quadrangle with library to the left

The Planning Process

Moving a School Library into the Twenty-First Century

By **KATHLEEN G. PUTNAM**

WHEN I JOINED THE BOARD OF DIRECTORS OF THE AGNES IRWIN SCHOOL, a private, all-girls institution in Rosemont, Pennsylvania, our meetings were held evenings in the upper school library. The library was built in the 1970s and consisted of two separate levels with glaring yellow concrete walls. Lighting, especially at night, was terrible. It was amazing that any studying took place there, let alone innovative thinking on the part of the board. It was a cold, poorly lit, depressing place.

By the time I became chair of the board, the administration and trustees of the school had concluded that the time had come to renovate the library. We had just completed a new lower school gymnasium—a project that had produced the school's first $1 million gift. Agnes Irwin, like so many all-female schools and universities, had been slow to cultivate its alumnae and parents for large-scale donations. But given the successful funding of the gymnasium, the school was ready to tackle the library.

Choosing an Architect

Originally, we planned to interview only local architectural firms for the project. But one of our trustees discovered a firm in Hastings-on-Hudson, New York, that specialized in private and public school library renovations, and we agreed to add that firm to our list.

Peter Gisolfi came down to Rosemont to meet with us and, once we heard his presentation, it was clear that he was the right architect for our project.

Include All Constituents

The project took two years to complete. We insisted on being inclusive in the design process, talking with all of our constituencies: faculty, administrators, parents, librarians, and most importantly, our students. There were numerous evening and weekend meetings, all of which were attended by the architects. They were a collaborative group, listening to everybody's needs and desires—some of them impractical, others beyond our budget. Even so, they managed to incorporate many of our suggestions into the design of the library.

A major factor in the planning process for an institution located in a residential area is to involve the immediate neighbors at the onset of the project. We reached out to all of the neighboring residents and held coffee and information sessions with them every step of the way. We addressed the entire construction phase: how the trucks, noise, traffic, and demolition would be timed and handled.

Because the library would be out of commission for more than a full academic year, we told the neighbors we would rent trailers to house some of the books (most of the collection had to be put into storage) and also serve as makeshift study spaces. The trailers would be located in our parking lot, and we admitted that no matter how sleek they were, the trailers were not particularly attractive. We listened to the neighbors' concerns, and we did our best to minimize the inconvenience to them. These sessions were valuable, especially when it came time for us to present our plans to Radnor Township. We were able to show the township a united front, with few objections. This was vital to obtaining the necessary permits and approvals from the commissioners.

Technology and Environment

One of the challenges we faced was how to incorporate newly emerging technology into the library. We needed to integrate the necessary wiring into the design without it becoming intrusive or ugly. One of the lead architects came up with the perfect solution: he designed tables so that the wires could be threaded from under the floor up through the legs. The tables were handsome as well as technologically functional.

In addition to the study spaces, we wanted to include a reading area with comfortable chairs, a place where a student could curl up with a book. This space in our library is located on the stairwell landing between the lower level of book stacks and the upper level of study areas. To this day, students love to relax in the overstuffed chairs in front of the fireplace to do their reading, whether required or recreational.

Honoring One of Our Own

The library was dedicated to and named for our then-head of school, Margaret Penney Moss. Penney had spent nearly all of her academic career at Agnes Irwin, except for a brief time at the Bryn Mawr School in Baltimore. She was a teacher, middle school head, assistant headmistress, interim head of the school, and finally head of the school. Except for her students, Penney was devoted to books and reading more than anything. It was an easy decision to name our new library the Margaret Penney Moss Upper School Library. At the ribbon-cutting ceremony, we celebrated both the new space and the woman for whom it had been named.

Kathleen G. Putnam served on the board of trustees of the Agnes Irwin School for twelve years, including three years as chair.

New connecting stair and mezzanine. Inset: Original stair.

The Impact

Connecting a Library of Separate Spaces

By **PETER GISOLFI**

THE AGNES IRWIN SCHOOL, AN INDEPENDENT DAY school for girls, was founded in 1869 on an eighteen-acre site in Rosemont, Pennsylvania. Rosemont is one of the communities located along the commuter railroad line that serves the prosperous western suburbs of Philadelphia. The school accommodates approximately 650 girls, from pre-kindergarten through twelfth grade.

The upper school library was constructed in the 1960s in an austere building that featured interior walls and ceilings of exposed, reinforced concrete. The library was located on two levels, with little connection between them; each level functioned as a separate space, joined to the other by a narrow stairway.

Program of Space Requirements

The building committee included the president and vice president of the board of trustees, the head of the school, the head of development, and the school's two librarians. By walking through the library with the committee members and discussing the opportunities and constraints of the building, the program of space requirements evolved:

- Transform the 6,500-square-foot upper school library so that the two levels function as one space.
- Create a library that can be run by two librarians—perhaps one upstairs and one downstairs—with sight lines that allow each librarian to see nearly the whole library.

- Transform the library to accommodate a 25 percent increase in the student population.
- Accommodate new technologies and systems for current needs, and allow for flexibility in the future.

Design Objectives

Through extensive discussions with the building committee, we established the following design objectives:

- Use more refined interior finishes so that the appearance of the library corresponds to other campus buildings.
- Develop an interior architectural language that suggests permanence, tranquility, and scholarship.
- Use the new finishes and new architectural language to create a unified library.
- Make the library more transparent internally, and to the rest of the school and campus.

New Plan

We investigated several options to visually connect the two main levels of the library. Ultimately, we returned to our original concept, which called for cutting an opening in the floor of the upper level to allow visibility to the level below. We later enhanced that visibility by designing a mezzanine-level read-

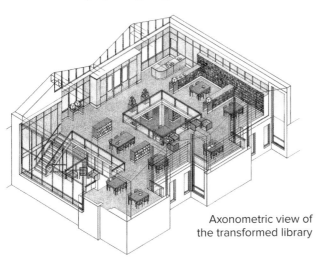

Axonometric view of the transformed library

ing lounge, adjacent to an outside glass wall. All three levels are linked by generously sized open stairs with glass railings. The transformed library was equipped with the electronic and digital features of the era.

The new three-level interior space provides a more refined, modernist environment by introducing ash paneling, slatted acoustical ceilings, limestone bases, muted carpeting, customized task lamps and ceiling fixtures, and cherry tables and seating. The plan creates a welcoming and more spacious library within the original footprint.

Collaborative Strategies

Successful collaboration gives the owner a voice in the design process. The building committee met frequently and critiqued alternative design alternatives.

- A relatively small committee of active participants allowed for productive discussions.
- By establishing clear objectives early in the process, we were able to reach agreement on design and construction issues with ease.
- The committee members remained cheerful and upbeat throughout the deliberations; this enabled open communication.

Achieving Success

The Agnes Irwin library became one of the school's most active communal spaces; it supports independent research and collaborative study. The new three-level library feels like one space. The exposed concrete surfaces are gone; they have been replaced by interior finishes that are harmonious, and that reflect the ample daylight provided by glass walls and clerestory windows.

Because of the new, more open arrangement, library usage has increased dramatically. Transparency from level to level makes passive observation of the students easy and unobtrusive.

Main reading room

The Impact

Two-Level Library Accommodates Multiple Activities Simultaneously

By **JULIE DIANA**

THE ENROLLMENT OF THE UPPER SCHOOL DIVISION at the Agnes Irwin School has increased by 30 percent in the past fifteen years. As a result, the school often lacks adequate space for large-scale social gatherings and group projects. The M. Penney Moss Library provides seating for about eighty students. During lunch, study, and club periods, nearly every seat in the library is taken. It is a common meeting spot for academic and extracurricular work and is regarded as the social heart of the high school.

The upper school library is a bright, attractive place for individual study and group work. By scheduling a class on each floor of the two-level library, multiple classes can be accommodated at the same time. In addition to well-lighted worktables for collaborative study, there is plenty of comfortable seating in lounge areas on the upper and mezzanine levels.

The library provides ample space for the display of special collections and new materials. Over the years, our reference collection has shifted to online databases, and we have reduced the size of that collection. At the same time, we have increased the fiction stacks, which now house an up-to-date young adult collection, including a large selection of graphic novels.

During the change of classes on school days, the stairway that connects the two floors of the library via the mezzanine lounge has become one of the most-used pathways in the school. With direct access to this increased traffic flow, the librarians are able to attract students with book displays, contests that promote recreational reading, and other outreach programming.

Although the library is a popular gathering place, the design does not always respond to the needs of today's student and faculty users. When the original library was redesigned, students mostly worked on projects individually, whereas current projects are more likely to require collaborative work in small groups or teams. Today's libraries need spaces that support and encourage collaborative work, such as alcoves, glass-enclosed conference rooms, and flexible furnishings and seating.

In addition, many newer libraries include instructional spaces that are large enough to accommodate a full classroom of students. At the time our library was redesigned, classroom-size instructional space was not included. As a result, some instruction that might better take place in our library takes place in a classroom.

Quiet Study vs. Collaborative Work

The Moss Library is an inviting open space. It is often used for student and faculty gatherings, class meetings, and social events. However, a two-story space can be challenging for supervision and sound control. The cutout in the floor unifies the two levels and provides sight lines between them, but without defined alcoves or small conference rooms, it is difficult for quiet study and collaborative work to take place at the same time. In general, libraries are transitioning from areas devoted mostly to individual study to those that cater to more collaborative work. In so doing, these libraries include the vibrant spaces that our users love. Nevertheless, we still need to address the quiet library expectations of some members of our school community.

Advice for Planning a New Library

Although I was not a member of the staff when the new library at the upper school was planned, I offer the following advice, based on my experience using the space:

DESIGN TEAM
Peter Gisolfi
Frank Craine
Vladimir Rigueur
Diane Collins
Wing Koo
Garth McIntosh

PHOTOGRAPHY BY
Tom Bernard

- Ask the entire school community for input. The design should not reflect the vision of the library staff alone. Students will have ideas for creative use of the space that librarians, teachers, and administrators may not have considered. This might be a way to use the collaborative design process with students.
- Address the needs of students for individual work and also for downtime, socializing, and collaborative learning.
- Is your library currently serving needs that can be better served by other spaces in your school? For instance, if the library hosts large study halls, perhaps the cafeteria or a group instruction room could be used for this purpose. This could free up library space for other uses.
- Make your library a welcoming destination with an area furnished with comfortable seating for socializing. Our library uses the mezzanine for informal lounging.
- Large windows create bright, sunlit spaces, and also create transparency from the outside to the inside. Similarly, glass walls and glass door panels can serve to interest passersby in activities occurring throughout the library.
- Positioning the library in a central location with multiple entrances establishes the space as one of the main public areas of the school; this invites students to visit the library and spend more time there.

Julie Diana is director of libraries and humanities innovation at the Agnes Irwin School.

Main reading room after transformation

The new central stair connects all levels in the building and is transparent to the library.

chapter 10

The Planning Process

Creating a Coherent School from Multiple Acquisitions

By **STEPHEN M. CLEMENT, III**

EVENTUALLY, I CAME TO UNDERSTAND WHY I WASN'T SHOWN THE SCHOOL'S library when I was a candidate for the job as the Browning School's new headmaster in 1988. I had met the search committee at an elegant, art-filled apartment on Park Avenue, and I engaged with the faculty at a well-orchestrated session in the school's most recently improved large space. But I realized after I accepted the job, which was offered over lunch at a posh Fifth Avenue men's club, that I had never been given a stem-to-stern tour of the school itself.

The Browning School had just recognized its centennial, celebrating its storied past. Founded in 1888 by John D. Rockefeller, who was in the process of moving his family from Cleveland to New York, the first "school" was actually a tutoring group for four adolescent boys, including John D. Rockefeller Jr. The headmaster chosen was John Aaron Browning, a recent graduate of Columbia College, who had majored in the classics; he lived at the Dakota on West 72nd Street and Central Park West. Browning's school quickly grew and thrived, and in 1922, the trustees moved it from its original site at 31 West 55th Street

to their own building at 52 East 62nd Street, between Madison and Park avenues.

Like so many other independent schools in Manhattan in the first half of the twentieth century, Browning faced the task of fitting increasing numbers of children into tight spaces by stacking small classrooms on top of each other. Additional challenges of the age included the Great Depression's drain on tuition dollars and salaries, the shortage of male teachers due to military service during World War II, and threats of the Cold War that might limit free speech. My predecessor once observed that the trustees "almost sold the building to the Russians." Over the years, the school had acquired an adjacent carriage house and, eventually, an eight-story apartment building. A rooftop gym was added to the original school building. For financial reasons, the top half of the apartment building was sold to the tenants.

When I finally did a thorough tour of "my" new school in the summer of 1988, I found a poorly maintained facility scattered over three building lots with close to fifteen floor levels and few logical paths leading from A to B, let alone A to Z. The thought of dropping seeds or scattering breadcrumbs so that I could retrace my route was not entirely out of the question.

Interestingly, the library was located at the heart of the school, in this case the sole location where one could pass directly through all three buildings with a minimal number of level changes. Maximum disruption in the library, however, occurred every forty-five minutes because all the boys and all the teachers in the school trooped through the space from one class to the next. Because of New York City fire codes, the library doors were solid and could not be propped open, and one never knew what to expect when entering closed doors.

I often found the librarian listening intently with a tiny transistor radio at his ear. He was a Yankees fan. When he wasn't supervising, he was out on the street smoking. Boys unsupervised were at times tussling. Clearly something had to be done.

The first construction project of my headship, however, was completely uninspiring: the renovation of all the boys' bathrooms. The bathroom walls were covered with tiles one shade darker than calamine lotion, and while the pink color seemed an odd choice for a boys' school, legend had it that the tiles had been available en masse on the cheap. At the end of the final board meeting in June 1989, I led the trustees, mostly parents, on a tour of the facilities. "This, ladies and gentlemen, is what your boys use many times a day." An upgrade was approved on the spot, and gleaming white tiles with a thin red accent band greeted the boys the following year.

After the bathrooms, other projects were tackled, and a new library was at the head of the list. In the mid-1990s, the school expanded into two floors of the adjacent apartment building (referred to as "40 East"), enabling a library to be built on the third floor. The Henry Bradley Martin Library included study carrels, book stacks, office space, a

Students in the new upper school library

Computer stations in the new upper school library

junior library, and a small computer lab. Interestingly, the lab, the gift of the family of an IBM heir, was equipped with early Macs.

In the decades of the 1990s and the 2000s, the city and the school thrived. Successful endowment campaigns were undertaken, the school's enrollment grew from under 300 to over 400, and Browning became increasingly selective and more desirable as one of only two all-boys, K-through-12, independent schools in Manhattan. Browning also became a leader in the International Boys' Schools Coalition. However, despite many small construction projects, which took place almost every summer, the total physical plant was not suitable in the twenty-first century for a school with almost 500 people using it daily.

This is where Peter Gisolfi came in.

Peter and I had been classmates at Yale, and while we did not know each other at the time, I became aware of his deftness and skills at one of our major class reunions. At Yale's reunions, all of us were housed in Timothy Dwight, a residential college built in the Colonial Revival style in the 1930s. Peter led his former classmates through renovations he had created at the college, especially the common spaces of the library and dining halls.

I liked both Peter's design aesthetic and his low-key but definitive leadership style. I also learned that he had performed years of renovations at the lofty University Club on Fifth Avenue in New York. If he was good enough for James Gamble Rogers and McKim Mead and White, he'd be good enough for Browning.

I told the Browning trustees about my classmate. They concurred, fund-raising commenced, financing was arranged, and we were off on our five-year saga. I was the complex project's cheerleader in chief, and I loved the role. With the finished product, the Browning Library was back at the heart of the school. Wrapped in glass, the library encompasses three floor levels that flow logically and gracefully, and lead to a lovely landscaped reading terrace. The magic of the finished product is that it looks as though it has always been there. Only Peter and I can now recall all of the twists and turns that led to its creation, and over drinks at the Yale Club, we agreed to forget all of the travail. From seeds on the floor and transistor radios at the ear, he has led us a long way.

Stephen M. Clement, III was headmaster of the Browning School from 1988 to 2016.

The Design

A Small Academic Library Accommodates a Range of Student Needs

By **PETER GISOLFI**

THE BROWNING SCHOOL IS LOCATED ON EAST 62ND Street in New York City, west of Park Avenue. When our firm started working on the Browning School project, the building was a confusing and illegible group of spaces located in three adjacent buildings on twelve levels: the original school building from 1922 on the east side, a narrow building in the center from the 1950s, and the lower five floors of a 1912 apartment building on the west side.

The Browning School is a K-through-12 college preparatory school for boys, founded in 1888. The current enrollment is approximately 400 students, with 40 to 50 students graduating each year.

Program of Space Requirements

The program of space requirements for the library is unusual. Because of the small size of the school, students from ages 5 through 18 had used the same library. The planning decision made by the school administration and trustees was to move the library from a remote location on the third floor to a visible location on the first floor. Within the confines of the new location, a variety of library spaces had to be accommodated: a separate space for upper school students, a separate space for lower school students, shared activity space, an outdoor reading terrace, and a maker space. The combination of these spaces adds up to 3,200 square feet.

Design Objectives

- The most compelling design objective was to create a legible arrangement for the entire school, one that could be understood by the staff, students, and even visitors.
- The second objective was to emphasize transparency by using glass walls where possible, and generously sized glass panels in all classroom and office doors.
- The third objective was to visually connect the library to the more public realm of the building, including the main lobby, the gymnasium, the dining hall, and the central stairway.

New Plan

The plans for the overall building of 50,000 square feet and the library of 3,200 square feet are by necessity intertwined. The new building diagram focuses on three staircases, two of which are new.

The most important feature is the central staircase, which is located adjacent to a south-facing glass wall (in the narrow, central building). The other two stairs are located at the east and west ends of the building.

The library, situated on two building levels, is adjacent to the entry lobby and the central, transparent stairway. Because of the split-level arrangement of the connected buildings, the central staircase actually connects ten levels. The most important public spaces—the entry lobby, the gymnasium, the library, and the dining hall—are visible to each other and mostly visible to anyone entering the main lobby.

The multilevel layout of the library helps to organize the spaces for younger and older students. The upper level includes the shared, flexible space and access to the outdoor reading terrace to the south. This is adjacent to the space assigned to the younger children, separated by a glass wall. At the lower level (one half flight down) are spaces devoted to the older students for individual and collaborative

Maker space in the library

Original first floor

LEGEND

CIRCULATION

GATHERING SPACE

CLASSROOM

SPECIAL CLASSROOM

ADMINISTRATION

ATHLETIC SERVICES

SERVICE

OUTDOOR SPACE

North

0   8   16   32

Transformed first floor

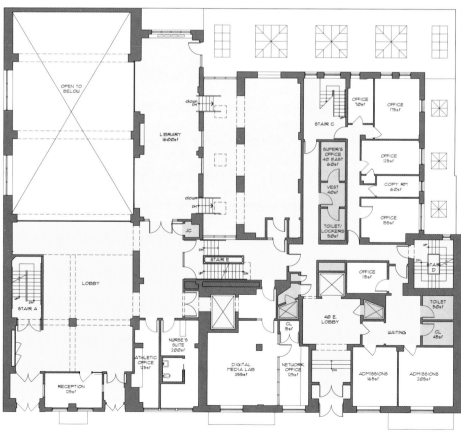

work. A small reading nook on the lower level is located next to the internal stair, which connects the two levels of the library. Across the central stair hallway at the lower level is the maker space, which is separated acoustically from the rest of the library.

Collaborative Strategies

The building design committee included the head of the school, heads of the three school divisions (lower school, middle school, and upper school), the business manager, three trustees, the owners' representative, and the architects. During the numerous design review meetings, the head of the school, Stephen Clement III, exercised a gentle yet perceptive authority. Meetings were held every Wednesday at 8 a.m. In addition, we made periodic presentations to the board of trustees.

To understand the special needs of the school, such as the lower school, the sciences, the music spaces, and so on, we met with representatives of each discipline. For the library, we met repeatedly with the head librarian, Sarah Murphy, who was an enthusiastic and persuasive participant.

We started the planning and design work in September 2011, and within three to four months, the transformative plan for the building had evolved. A major challenge was how to build a new school and new library while the building was occupied by students and faculty. The solution was to start construction each May, as the school year was winding down, and to continue working in the summer and early fall throughout the five-year duration of the project.

During the first summer, we began a partial renovation of the gymnasium, and installed the first glass wall, which allowed for transparency, with acoustical separation, between the lobby and the gymnasium. This move set the stage for future transparency between the lobby and the library. All of the construction work was completed in five elongated summers, and the entire school was transformed.

Achieving Success

Working collaboratively, the building committee succeeded in meeting the challenges presented by the space requirements and design objectives.

- The building is successful; it is organized and legible.
- The central, transparent stair drives the design solution.
- The main communal spaces, including the library, are visible from the entry lobby.
- There is an easy synergy across the central stair from the library on the south to the maker space on the north.
- The public connections of the lobby, the library, and the central stair give new importance to these functions.
- Although the library's physical space is tight, it is perceived as larger, owing to its transparency with the adjacent space. In essence, the library borrows space from its neighbor.
- Remarkably, students of all ages thrive in this small library.

New central stair ties together three existing buildings (Courtesy of K. Tanner)

Central staircase with view to the library

Storytime area with view of the reading terrace to the south

The Impact

A Quiet Gem Becomes a Destination

By **SARAH MURPHY**

PRIOR TO THE PHYSICAL TRANSFORMATION OF THE Browning School, the library was a hidden gem: we were tucked away on the second floor, full of sunshine and frequent solitude. Students—those who were assigned to classes or study halls with us, or those with free time—knew exactly where the library was and what it contained, but the broader community of faculty, staff, parents, and alumni were uncommon visitors. They would come if invited or if they needed our services, but we were unaccustomed to drop-ins or spur-of-the-moment browsers.

With the overall replanning of the building, it was quickly decided that the library should move from our quiet corner on the second floor to the first floor, near the main entrance. As plans were made, it became clear to me that not just the aesthetics, but the whole relationship of the physical library to the rest of the building and the commu-

nity was about to change. Our new library, with its glass doors and windows overlooking the gymnasium and lobby, is one of the first places seen when entering the building. Its two entrances, both from the glass-enclosed stair and the corridors, encourage people to drop by at all hours. We have now become the intellectual and physical heart of the school.

With increased visibility, parents and caregivers of our younger students feel free to stop in at the afternoon pickup, helping to form stronger relationships between librarians and families. Our colleagues are more likely to swing by on their way in or out of the building, or during a rare moment of downtime. We no longer have to issue specific invitations to teachers; their casual visits often lead to unexpected interdisciplinary projects. For instance, a science teacher dropped by on her way home recently and picked up one of our newest acquisitions, a picture book about identifying animals by their droppings. A new second-grade science unit was born. Our student patrons, too, have benefited from our new location, frequently making the library their first stop on the way into school or the last stop on their way out. We do miss our second-floor solitude every now and again, but the advantages of a central, transparent location far outweigh a few minutes of quiet.

One Space for K–12 Learners

The biggest challenge for any library in our building was going to be the use of space; the building is small and serves 400 students in grades K through 12. It was important to the librarians and to the architects that all ages were considered in the design of the space and that, to the degree possible in 3,200 square feet, we have designated spaces for different kinds of learning.

New outdoor reading terrace

From the lobby, a visitor walks into our main library area, which houses the reference and circulation desk, a row of desktop computers with quick access to printers, a small chess table (always occupied), and tables ideal for collaborative student work or meetings with teachers. During certain class times, these tables and chairs transform into a classroom. A large retractable screen supports our work in media literacy or library classes and can even turn the room into a screening space. Short shelving units surround the space, and this is where our small print reference collection lives. This large, multipurpose space is almost always busy, with a variety of ages being represented at once. Our proximity to the tech lab and maker space means that students seeking support or working on projects frequently travel back and forth.

A door at the back of the main space leads to a long, narrow terrace. Schools with campuses may take outdoor space for granted, but for a small Manhattan school, this access to fresh air and light is an oasis. In nice weather, it provides a spot for older students to congregate socially without disturbing library classes. Younger students see access to the terrace as a privilege and an ideal place for reading.

Since the school fits into what were once three separate buildings, each floor consists of two levels. Because of the placement of the library, patrons descend four steps to enter our lower level, first passing through our periodicals nook. Floor-to-ceiling glass connects this comfortable seating area to the building's main staircase and gives passersby a glimpse into the life of the library. The morning's newspapers and our robust periodical collection are housed here. A popular place for faculty seeking peace, this is the spot in the library where reading for pleasure is most likely to happen.

Most of the books are housed on the perimeter of the lower level. Shorter shelving units, on top of which new books can be displayed, separate three distinct study areas. This space, although only about twelve feet from the main library area, feels very different in both purpose and tone. The privacy of the working areas lends itself to intense study, so this space is primarily used as a quiet section for our older students. Collaborative work usually occurs upstairs, preserving the focus on our lower level.

The librarians all agree that our favorite spot in the new space is the Lower School Library, which is situated on the upper level between the main space and the quiet area below. It is entirely enclosed, but interior glass on three sides gives a feeling of openness and connection to the larger space. The fourth wall is a large floor-to-ceiling window that looks out onto the terrace. Adjacent to the window is my favorite library feature, a small recessed seating area where we hold K-through-4 library classes, as well as my weekly upper school advisory. It reminds us a bit of a tiny indoor amphitheater, but when a student said it looked like a hot tub, we settled on that. The boys sit around the steps of the "hot tub" for storytimes or to view lessons or videos on the nearby smart TV. The space is cozy and conducive to group conversation. Adjacent to the hot tub are the shelves holding our lower school collection—just the right height for small patrons. These shelves also provide ample space for displays of featured titles and new books.

In addition to the multitude of academic ways the students use the various spaces, our new central location has turned us into an event destination. We host evening book clubs and faculty gatherings; a number of student clubs use the space before school opens, and our parents association has hosted parties here. The space is flexible enough to support uses well beyond the curricular. In bringing visitors into the space, we are able to show off our collection and resources to a broad range of potential users and supporters.

Recommendations for Contributing to the Design Process

- Explore other spaces, especially those that are similar in size. Visiting expansive campus libraries just made me envious but visiting tiny city schools provided ideas and inspiration.
- Choose what is most important and advocate for that. You won't get everything you want, so decide what's worth fighting for. In our case, this was the recessed seating area in the lower school room. We saw something similar in another library, and the architects immediately understood and ran with the idea.
- Librarians' needs don't always match up with institutions' needs, or even patrons' needs. In our case, we sacrificed storage and office space for more square footage for patrons.
- Start weeding now. Whether you're losing shelf space or not, a move or a reopening is a great opportunity to make sure your collection is current, comprehensive, and used by your patrons. In small libraries this is even more essential, but it takes time to do it right. Begin this important work as early as possible in the process in order to avoid anxiety later.

DESIGN TEAM
Peter Gisolfi
Michael Tribe
Danny Lam
Belle Chen-Taylor

PHOTOGRAPHY BY
Robert Mintzes

Our old space was the first library I managed, and it was hard for me to part with the sunshine and the solitude, as well as the memories. But in reflecting on the new space, it is difficult to remain nostalgic. Our new library is fresh and adaptive to our students' needs. Without eschewing our mission of supporting curricula and information literacy as well as providing students with a collection of pleasure reading at all levels, our library and library program have been transformed in extraordinary and unanticipated ways.

Sarah Murphy is head librarian at the Browning School.

CONCLUSION
Creating the Essential Library

LIBRARIES HAVE BEEN AN IMPORTANT PART OF AMERICAN LIFE SINCE THE NINETEENTH CENTURY. The first libraries were designed to be inspiring—almost ecclesiastical—spaces that held valuable books and information. The library was a place of quiet and awe. Yet, as recently as 10 or 15 years ago, I was told that the use of e-readers to download books from the Internet would make public libraries obsolete, and that Google and other search applications on computers, tablets, and smartphones would displace academic libraries. These predictions could not have been more wrong. I am no longer hearing about the demise of libraries, and in fact, public, school, and academic libraries alike are busier and more essential than ever.

What has changed? In public libraries, the collection is no longer the main focus. Public libraries are places for social interaction and collaborative learning, as well as for quiet reading. In design, they seek a blend of large activity spaces, small group study areas, and places for individual reading. They have emerged as community cultural centers, places where a variety of intellectual, artistic, and social activities flourish for all ages.

At secondary schools and colleges, the library is often a social hub as well as a research center. Academic libraries support individual study and also feature classrooms and group workspaces that encourage collaboration. Successful school libraries are essential for learning. Here, students learn the techniques of research that extend beyond the quick fixes they can find on their digital devices.

Neither public, school, nor academic libraries are quiet spaces. They embrace the communal areas for gathering and working together on projects that were discouraged in the quiet libraries of the past. They seek openness and transparency in order to encourage participation, motivating onlookers to become involved. Yet every library is unique because each has its own physical setting and its own culture.

When I think back to the libraries we designed twenty years ago, and I compare them to the ideas incorporated into library design today, I see a shift in purpose. And I realize, too, that change was inevitable then, just as it is now. Libraries will continue to change—to adapt to new technologies and intentions—even as we are designing them.

General Principles and Specific Trends

In reviewing the ten examples presented in this book—five public libraries and five school and academic libraries—we can identify general principles and current trends that apply to contemporary library design and operation.

GENERAL PRINCIPLES

- The configuration of spaces influences the way the library is operated and used.
- The determining factors in the design of a library are the program of space requirements and the design objectives.
- The library must be flexible in order to accommodate various uses and arrangements, and must be adaptable to future change.

CURRENT TRENDS

- Libraries today are welcoming places with a design focus on openness and transparency.
- Libraries are interactive rather than separate and compartmentalized.
- By embracing technology—RFID, OPAC, material-handling systems, and so on—libraries have become more efficient, freeing librarians to be flexible and more helpful to patrons.

- With many books and resources digitized, the collections are smaller, giving libraries options to provide more spaces for reading and working within the collections.
- Collaborative projects are encouraged; alcoves, meeting rooms, and other enclosed spaces provide acoustic separation.
- Cafés, art galleries, and other informal spaces encourage gathering and socializing.
- As cultural centers, libraries provide programs, instruction, and engaging events for children, teens, and adults. The community rooms in many libraries are in use every day for activities as varied as exercise classes, storytimes, films, lectures, dramatic presentations, and musical performances.
- Today's libraries are often models of sustainable practice—positive examples for their communities.
- Earlier libraries were inspirational buildings that celebrated the essence of books and learning, and the permanence and continuity of important public institutions. Modern library design retains aspects of these characteristics while providing a more communal setting and greater flexibility.

Whether you build a new library or transform an existing one, do not build the best library of the previous era. Create an environment that facilitates new patterns of interaction, learning, and accessing information. Libraries are not created in a vacuum. Administrators, trustees, board members, librarians, community residents, faculty, students, and architects must work together—must collaborate—to arrive at the plan that best responds to the community that the library serves.

—*Peter Gisolfi*

INDEX